Methodologies for Analyzing Public Policies

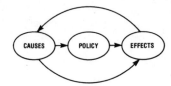

Policy Studies
Organization Series

Methodologies for Analyzing Public Policies

Frank P. Scioli, Jr.
Thomas J. Cook
University of Illinois,
    Chicago

Lexington Books
D.C. Heath and Company
Lexington, Massachusetts
Toronto   London

Library of Congress Cataloging in Publication Data

Main entry under title:

Methodologies for analyzing public policies.

Includes index.
1. Policy sciences—Methodology. I. Scioli, Frank P. II. Cook,
Thomas J.
H61.M492   309.2   75-8152
ISBN 0-669-00596-7

Copyright © 1975 by D.C. Heath and Company

Third printing, April 1979

Published simultaneously in Canada

Printed in the United States of America

International Standard Book Number: 0-669-00596-7

Library of Congress Catalog Card Number: 75-8152

Contents

Preface

Our major objective in developing this text is to advance the conduct of research in the field of public policy, with the goal of this research being the development of public policy that is effective in meeting the needs of society. A fundamental prerequisite for achieving these ends is that students of public policy possess the necessary methodological skills for careful analysis of substantive public policy. The collection of articles in this book is meant as a starting point in that direction.

Our intent is to be representative rather than exhaustive, and we urge more intensive investigation where in-depth skills in a particular methodology are desired. The references accompanying the various articles in the book provide instructive guideposts for further reading and study.

We are grateful for the cooperation we have received from each of the contributing authors. A special thanks also to Mike McCarroll and Penny Rohrbach at Lexington Books, who have been most helpful and thus greatly facilitated our producing this text.

**Methodologies for
Analyzing Public Policies**

**Part I
Introduction**

1

The Interaction of Substance and Method in the Study of Public Policy

Thomas J. Cook and Frank P. Scioli, Jr.

The study of public policy is a complex endeavor that confronts the researcher with a series of decisions, on choices among alternatives, having both substantive and methodological implications. The policy analyst is rarely in a position to analyze comprehensively a complex policy question with the full assurance that all of the potentially relevant dimensions of the question have received sufficient attention. Rather, he or she is forced to choose among alternative substantive foci and methodological approaches. In a sense, he or she must narrow the analytical focus to a specific subset of the overall policy question and apply a methodology that he or she feels is the most technically sound, given the constraints of the environment within which the research is conducted. The diagram in Figure 1-1 summarizes the overall perspective we are suggesting.

In terms of substantive foci, the researcher may choose to analyze one or more of several aspects relevant to the study of public policy.[1] One aspect may be the source and nature of demands for the enactment of public policy. The interplay of both public and private interests as they attempt to influence the choice of policy alternatives by governmental officials and public agencies has long been a research concern of political scientists. Other scholars have focused their attention on the policy process, that is, an identification of the factors relevant to an understanding of the formulation and enactment of public policy. As in the case of policy demands, the search has been for commonalities in policy formulation and enactment across different policy areas and diverse governmental jurisdictions. In other words, does the policy process exhibit similar patterns of interaction (in terms of individual and organizational behavior) regardless of the policy environment (e.g., federal, state, or local), or are there different models of the process applicable under different conditions? For example, is the policy process more insulated from external pressures at the state than at the local level?

3

A relatively recent research focus has been the attempt by several scholars to isolate those variables that best explain differentials in policy "outputs" by governments at both the state and local level. Policy outputs, in this instance, is a synonomous term for dollar expenditures for various governmental services, such as highways, police protection, medical care, etc. Much of the research has centered on the relative explanatory power of "political-institutional" factors versus socioeconomic factors. While a rather large body of research has been generated within the policy output perspective, relatively little systematic research attention has been focused on an important related concern: policy implementation.[2] We know very little about the mechanisms that, at least in principle, link the expenditure of public resources with the actual delivery of public services to the target population of a policy. There is often an implicit assumption of a linkage between policy goals and objectives, policy outputs, and the nature and amount of service delivery. To wit, if city A spends more per capita for police protection than city B, city A must have "better" police protection, the assumption being that the mechanism for delivering police services (i.e. policy implementation) is constant for both cities. As yet, very little empirical research has directly addressed this type of assumption. The question of policy implementation may be relevant to a final area of substantive focus: the analysis of policy impacts. Policy impact analysis attempts to identify and measure systematically the consequences, if any, that result from a given policy action.[3] In other words, what changes in the sociophysical environment of the policy can validly be attributed to a given policy action. Did, for example, the "war on poverty" program, Operation Headstart, significantly affect the cognitive abilities of children who participated in the program? What would be the consequences (i.e., the impact) of a nationwide ban on the sale, manufacture, or possession of handguns? These are examples of the types of questions that the impact analyst would address, thus shifting the research focus from what causes policy (i.e., policy impact analysis) to what policy causes.

The researcher is also confronted with an array of methodological alternatives and issues endemic to various substantive foci. A conceptual framework must be developed that isolates the most important concepts for study and sets forth the network of interrelationships between concepts. For example, in a policy-impact study, the relationships between policy goals and objectives, policy actions

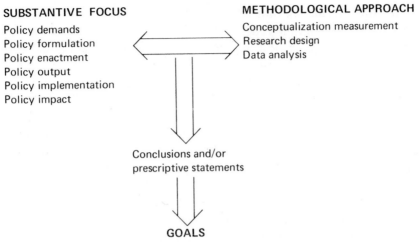

SUBSTANTIVE FOCUS

Policy demands
Policy formulation
Policy enactment
Policy output
Policy implementation
Policy impact

METHODOLOGICAL APPROACH

Conceptualization measurement
Research design
Data analysis

Conclusions and/or
prescriptive statements

GOALS

The development of an empirically
validated body of policy-relevant theory

and

the development of demonstrably
effective social policy which is
responsive to the needs of the citizenry

Figure 1-1. Public Policy Analysis

(i.e., program activities), and the behavior of impact criteria (e.g., performance indicators) require explication in terms of a set of causal hypotheses with specific empirical measures associated with the concepts of interest in the study. Thus, the question of concept formation and measurement procedures must be addressed early in the research study. The measurement issue involves a choice among alternative approaches towards establishing the objectivity, reliability, and validity of the empirical indicators selected to represent the concepts contained in the study. For example, in a study of policy implementation the concepts of "compliance" or "noncompliance" require explication in terms of objectively determined empirical measures, with evidence to support confidence in the reliability and validity of the measures. The same type of "choice" situation is present relative to selecting a research design and the accompanying data analysis procedures.

The design selected faces the test of controlling for the various threats to internal and external validity that are often present in public policy research.[4] In terms of internal validity, the researcher seeks the confidence that his or her results are not an artifact of the research design employed, or due to the presence of other factor(s) that mitigate against the acceptance of the research conclusions. External validity concerns the generalizability of the research findings from one research locale to other research settings, an important question relative to building a cumulative body of policy-relevant research. In dealing with the issues of internal and external validity, the researcher is again faced with a number of design alternatives from which to choose, ranging from a randomized experiment to a nonexperimental design perspective.

While the research design ultimately selected narrows the range of choices relative to data analysis approaches, the policy analyst is still faced with choosing an approach, and related statistical techniques, that dredge the maximum amount of policy relevant information from the data. As in any research effort, the attempt is to utilize an approach that is consistent with the measurement properties and collection procedures represented in the data. The misuse of statistical techniques is an all too common occurrence in the social sciences. For the policy analyst, there is an additional concern: fitting the data analysis to the intended, or potential, audience for the research. For many social scientists, there is a temptation to ''over-analyze'' the data through the application of highly sophisticated multivariate statistical techniques, thus rendering the research study incomprehensible to the public administrator, or public official, who must make decisions of a more practical, and less ''academic,'' nature. The shelves of more than one public agency are full of research reports that may be exemplars of methodological ''overkill'' relative to the decision-making needs of the audience for whom the research was conducted. Thus, there is a need for data analysis that is both technically sound *and* relevant to the decision-making concerns of public officials, as well as to the interests of the more traditional academic audience.

A final issue concerns the output of a policy analysis study. As was alluded to above, the potential audience for an increasing amount of policy research is of a nonacademic nature, such as public administrators and elected officials. The interest within this ''practitioner'' audience is decidedly for prescriptive statements tied to recommended courses of action, rather than for conclusions that relate to theory development within a particular academic discipline. While this is not mainly a substantive or methodological issue, it does bear on the type of information generated by a research study and the form in which this information is presented: prescriptive statements vs. theoretically relevant conclusions. This is not meant to suggest that the two types of research output are mutually exclusive, rather to point out the issue and to suggest its consideration by the researcher. Hopefully, future policy research will produce results that are relevant to the interests of both types of audiences, public administrators and discipline-oriented academicians.[5]

This research will, in our judgment, best be undertaken with two major goals as guidance: the development of an empirically validated body of policy-relevant theory *and* the development of demonstrably effective social action policy, that is, policy actions that are responsive in meeting citizen needs. It is our view that it is time for the study of public policy to move beyond the concerns of particular academic disciplines and raise the more general issue of the value of policy research for identifying effective policy actions that have a significant impact on social problems. In clarifying some of the methodological alternatives and issues that potentially confront the policy analyst, we hope that this book represents a positive step towards both goals.

Notes

1. For an introduction to the public policy field see: Thomas R. Dye, *Understanding Public Policy,* 2nd ed. (Englewood Cliffs, N.J.: Prentice-Hall, Inc., 1975); Charles O. Jones, *An Introduction to the Study of Public Policy* (Belmont, Calif.: Wadsworth Publishing Co., 1970); James E. Anderson, *Public Policy Making* (New York: Praeger Publishers, 1975).

2. See: Anderson, *Public Policy Making* pp. 98-131; Martin Rein and Francine Rabinowitz, "Implementation: a Theoretical Perspective," May, 1974 (Duplication); Jeffrey Pressman and Aaron Wildavsky, *Implementation* (Berkeley, Calif.: University of California Press, 1973).

3. Thomas J. Cook and Frank P. Scioli, Jr., "A Research Strategy for Analyzing the Impacts of Public Policy," *Administrative Science Quarterly* 17 (September 1972), pp. 328-40.

4. Thomas J. Cook and Frank P. Scioli, Jr., "Impact Analysis in

Public Policy Research,'' in Kenneth Dolbeare, ed., *Yearbook of Politics & Public Policy* (Beverly Hills, Calif.: Sage Publications, Inc., forthcoming 1976).

5. James S. Coleman, *Policy Research in the Social Sciences* (Morristown, N.J.: General Learning Press, 1972), pp. 2-4.

Part II
Measurement

Introduction to Part II

Some analysts would argue that the validity of a research investigation ultimately rests upon the measurement procedures that underlie the data base contained in the study. Thus, a poorly conceived and improperly administered measurement procedure precludes the possibility of valid results, and, hence, negates the utility of the study as a source of decision-relevant information. We tend to agree with this position and are most sensitive to questions concerning the extent to which measurement procedures are standardized, objective, reliable, and, most importantly, valid.

The chapters in Part II address the measurement question from a variety of perspectives: Chapter 2 by Elinor Ostrom and chapter 3 by David A. Caputo stress the need for multiple indicators of policy relevant concepts, with special reference to assessing the actual extent of service delivery associated with various substantive policy areas. The final selection, chapter 4 by Eugene Meehan, questions the analytical utility of a current research area, social indicator research, and suggests an alternative approach towards the measurement of policy-relevant concepts employing a public choice perspective. While much of the discussion is cast within a policy-evaluation framework, the emphasis upon clarity in conceptualization and attention to measurement standards apply across all substantive areas of policy research.

2

The Need for Multiple Indicators in Measuring the Output of Public Agencies

Elinor Ostrom

The need for more valid and reliable means of measuring the output of government services at all levels of government is a critical problem for policy analysts. It is particularly important at the municipal level, where such outputs and their variations have the most direct impact upon citizens, and where sophisticated measurement and evaluation capabilities are least likely to be found. This need is easily documented by reference to (1) reports of service breakdowns contributing to the exodus of middle-class residents from central cities (without valid and reliable measures of services provided, how can we begin to estimate service levels required to stem or reverse this exodus?); (2) lawsuits contending infringement of the equal rights provisions of the constitution through discriminatory provisions of services (without valid and reliable measures of services provided, how can such cases be equitably resolved?); and (3) frequent calls for reorganization of governmental arrangements, particularly in metropolitan areas, in order to provide government services more efficiently (without more accurate measures of services provided, how can we establish the probable consequences of such reforms, or measure those consequences in cases where such reorganizations are carried out?).[1]

The task of measuring the output of most government agencies is far more difficult than that of measuring the output of private firms. The output of a private firm is defined as the total quantity of any product manufactured or produced over a period of time. The output of a private firm can frequently be measured in physical terms, such as the total cars produced a year or the total loaves of bread produced a day. The number of physical units produced is an acceptable measure for most purposes.

The author gratefully acknowledges the support of the RANN Division of the National Science Foundation in the form of Grant Number GI 38535; the author also appreciates the helpful comments given to an earlier draft of this chapter by Vernon Greene, John Hamilton, Jnana Hodson, Roger B. Parks, Nancy M. Neubert, Vincent Ostrom, Eric Scott, and Russ Youmans.

While the output of a private firm is frequently measured in terms of the physical units produced, the dollar value of the output is also used as a measure of output. Prices for private goods and services are established by *voluntary transactions* between buyers and sellers. Consumers voluntarily enter markets and decide whether and how much of a particular good to purchase from among the alternatives offered. A consumer unwilling to pay the market price for a good can be excluded from consuming its benefits. In deciding to buy or not to buy, a consumer must make some estimate of the value he will receive in the consumption process. A consumer will be willing to purchase a good only if he expects that the benefits he will receive, less the costs he will incur in consuming a good, exceed the net benefits he could obtain from using the purchase price in a different fashion. Thus, the dollar value of the output of a private firm determined by the prices at which units are sold includes a measure of both (1) the amount of output *and* (2) the expected value of the output *by the consumer*.

In the public sector it is much more difficult to conceptualize and measure either the physical output of a public agency or the appropriate dollar value of the output. What is the output, for example, of a police department? In a general sense, the output of the police is the maintenance of order, the prevention and detection of crime, the enforcement of the law, and the provision of emergency response services to citizens. One sees police on patrol and assumes that all individuals within some range of effects are benefited by this activity. However, the "production process" does not produce a clearly defined output and the lack of a market makes it difficult to know how much those effects are valued by those receiving them.

The outputs of many municipal agencies exhibit several characteristics of public goods.[2] In particular, the outputs are often indivisible and potential beneficiaries cannot easily be excluded from receiving the effects of the output. Street lighting, for example, cannot be provided to one resident of a block without simultaneously providing it to others living on the block or travelling along the block. The costs of excluding some from the benefit so that those who do benefit can be charged for the benefit would be very high. Given indivisibility and nonexcludability, the problem of measuring output pervades the analysis of all public policy related to the provision of municipal public services.[3]

The indivisibilities and lack of exclusion characteristic of public goods prevents reliance upon single measures such as quantity or dollar value of output. It becomes necessary to measure several aspects of public output simultaneously. Thus, the speed of response made by a local police department is one indicator of the service level being provided by the department. Sole reliance on such a single indicator as *the* measure of output, however, could lead to serious problems both for policy analysts and public actors.

The FBI Crime Index has too frequently been utilized as a single measure of the output of police agencies.[4] The problem of widespread nonreporting of crimes can be corrected to some extent by supplementing official FBI crime reports with other indicators of victimization derived from household sample surveys.[5] Further indicators of the output of police agencies can be obtained by asking recipients of police service about their specific experiences with and evaluations of local police services. The ratio of warrants issued to warrants applied for can be used as a comparative indicator of the performance of police departments served by the same prosecutor.[6] The geographic distribution of the sale of private protection devices can be used as a negative indicator of the sense of safety felt by citizens and their lack of reliance on the police for primary protection.

Employing any single indicator of public agency output as the basis for structuring internal incentive systems can lead to pathologies. Jerome Skolnick has graphically described one such pathology resulting from the excessive reliance upon "the clearance rate" by the Oakland Police Department as a measure of performance.[7] Detectives in the department were led to treat the most active and confirmed burglars, once arrested on a charge, as a potential resource of great value for future promotions. If the detective were able to offer a suspected burglar a sufficient reward in the form of significantly reduced charges, he might convince him to confess to a large number of crimes—thus "clearing" them all with a single arrest and a reduced charge.

Policy analysts can fall into the same trap by reliance upon single indicators. Far too many articles examining factors affecting the output of public agencies have utilized as their sole measure of output an absolute or relative input quantity such as total public expenditures or per capita public expenditures. The use of expenditures figures by social scientists as the sole measure of output has legitimized the growing reliance of the courts on similar indicators.

Recently, an important series of cases has been argued before the courts in which the basic issue has been the unequal distribution of public goods and services to particular neighborhoods based on alleged racial, ethnic, or economic discriminations.[8] Most of the cases focusing on the provision of educational services have utilized dollar resources per child as their measure of output.[9] James Coleman and others have challenged the adequacy of simple dollar expenditures levels as measures of the output of educational systems.[10] In several studies of police performance in the Indianapolis, Chicago, Grand Rapids, St. Louis, and Nashville metropolitan areas, the output of the police measured by a series of multiple indicators of performance has *not* been positively associated with average per capita expenditure levels by city.[11] Excessive reliance upon expenditure levels as the sole indicators of output may lead the courts into the position of finding the most wasteful (or most graft-ridden) cities providing the highest levels of output to their citizens.

Such methodological traps can be mitigated by the conscious development and reliance on multiple indicators of output derived wherever possible from multiple modes of data collection. Researchers at The Urban Institute have pioneered in this regard. They have explored a wide variety of potential indicators to be used simultaneously in any effort of measure output.[12]

The Workshop in Political Theory and Policy Analysis at Indiana University has recently embarked on a research effort for the RANN Division of the National Science Foundation. The major focus of this project is the development of multimode measurements of two municipal services: street lighting and street repair. For street lighting, we developed a method to utilize a precision light meter to record the level of night lighting on sidewalks and streets facing a particular block face.[13] For street repair, we developed a mechanical device, called the Residential Street Roughness Indicator, to measure the roughness of a street.[14] In addition, we also developed an observation form and procedure that can be used by trained observers to record specific data about various aspects of street condition.

In addition to the physical mode of data collection used for each of the service areas, we also utilized two other modes: a survey of respondents, and indicators derived from agency records. A pretest of our survey instrument was administered to respondents living in seven small neighborhoods in Indianapolis during 1974. A total of 326 respondents were interviewed in this test. Citizens were asked a series of questions to elicit their *perceptions* of street lighting and road repair, their *evaluations* of the same, and their *preferences* for differing levels of these services. Agency records provided our third mode of data collection. Unfortunately, we found this mode of data collection to be the most difficult of all. Agency records were so fragmentary that few consistent indicators could be developed. For road repair we were able to code the frequency of complaints directed to the Indianapolis Department of Transportation concerning the roads facing the respondents in our survey. For street lighting, we were not able to code much more than the frequency and pattern of street lights shown on agency maps.

Preliminary data analysis has been initiated. One of the first questions we have addressed is "What is the relationship between citizen perceptions of service levels and our unobtrusive measures of service levels?" This is a particularly important question since many policy analysts are hesitant to rely at all upon citizen reported evaluation of output due to the assumed inaccuracy of citizen perceptions of service levels. Early analysis does not provide a completely uniform picture of accurate perception across all indicators. However, the more specific and concrete the referent to which our questions were addressed, the more likely a high level of association exists between unobtrusive measures and citizen perceptions of service levels.

For example, in general, citizens were quite accurate in their perceptions concerning a number of specific aspects concerning the condition of street repair on their block face. Citizens accurately reported the type of street surface, the presence or absence of curbs, the condition of their curbs, the presence of surface disintegration, and the presence of potholes.[15]

Sue Carroll of the Workshop staff developed a roughness scale for each block face included in our study and for each quadrant of a block on which respondents lived.[16] The scale was composed of individual items coded for each quadrant of a block including amount of surface disintegration, number and size of potholes, presence or absence of cracks, presence or absence of bumps, and presence or absence of utility cuts. Each observer was also asked to rate each blockface as being "very rough," "fairly rough," "fairly smooth," and "very smooth." These observer ratings were strongly

Table 2-1
Measures of Association Between Citizen Perceptions of Roughness and Scores on Both the Quadrant and the Blockface Roughness Scales

	Entire Sample	Sex		Education			Age			
		Females	Males	Less Than High School Graduate	High School Graduate	More Than High School Graduate	Less Than 30 Yrs. Old	30-45 Yrs. Old	46-60 Yrs. Old	More Than 60 Yrs. Old
Association Between Perceptions and Scores on Quadrant Roughness Scale	gamma = 0.76 N > (247)	0.74 (142)	0.78 (102)	0.73 (82)	0.69 (77)	0.85 (80)	0.68 (80)	0.61 (66)	0.87 (57)	0.93 (44)
Association Between Perceptions and Scores on Blockface Roughness Scale	gamma = 0.76 N = (319)	0.71 (183)	0.81 (132)	0.72 (99)	0.71 (106)	0.80 (106)	0.67[a] (190)		0.89[a] (129)	

	Length of Residence			Length of Blockface		
	Less Than 1 Yr.	1-5 Yrs.	More Than 5 Yrs.	Short (<650 Ft.)	Medium (650-900 Ft.)	Long (>900 Ft.)
Association Between Perceptions and Scores on Quadrant Roughness Scale	0.66[a] (126)		0.89 (121)	0.81 (74)	0.85 (79)	0.44 (74)
Association Between Perceptions and Scores on Blockface Roughness Scale	0.67[a] (160)		0.87 (159)	Yule's Q= 0.91[b] (100)	Yule's Q = 0.69[b] (101)	Yule's Q = 0.69[b] (118)

[a]Because of the nature of the distributions, there were too few respondents to compute gamma for these categories separately. Therefore, two categories have been combined.

[b]Even by combining these two categories, there were so few respondents with scale scores placing them into the "very rough" or "fairly rough" scale categories that gamma could not be computed. Therefore, the scale was dichotomized into "rough" and "smooth" and Yule's Q was computed.

Source: From Sue Carroll, "An Analysis of the Relationship Between Citizen Perceptions and Unobtrusive Measures of Street Conditions" (Bloomington, Indiana: Indiana University, Department of Political Science, Workshop in Political Theory and Policy Analysis, Research Report Number 10), p. 28.

related to the "roughness scale" for both a quadrant (gamma = 0.94) and for the block face as a whole (gamma = 0.97). Given these high coefficients, the roughness scale derived from the individual items coded by observers would appear to have at least some face validity.

When respondents' perceptions of the roughness of the street on their block were then associated with the quadrant and blockface roughness scale, the measure of association between them is fairly strong (gamma = 0.76 for both scales). As shown in Table 2-1, some variation occurred across various control variables. Those persons with more than a high school diploma, those over 45, those who have lived on a block more than five years, and those living on medium to short blocks tended to be more "accurate" in their perceptions of road roughness. Initial data analysis with scores produced by the Residential Street Roughness Indicator device has produced consistent findings with those reported on here. There is a high association among all of these individual modes of data collection concerning the level of road roughness—individual respondent perception, the roughness scale computed from observer coding of street conditions, and the output from the mechanical device for measuring road roughness.

Although the levels of association are not, in general, as high as in the case of street conditions, statistically significant correlations between citizen perceived streetlight brightness levels on their blockface and data from a precision photoelectric meter were found.[17] Further, a distinct pattern emerged between the strength of association and the size of the interval on either side of a respondent's house over which light-meter readings were averaged. Correlations reach a maximum when meter readings are averaged over intervals relatively proximate to a respondent's home and decline as the meter readings are averaged over widening intervals. The lowest correlation is between citizen perceptions and light-meter readings averaged over the entire blockface. Indeed, for some subsets of the sample, this correlation was not statistically significant. Thus, citizens appear to show a pronounced tendency to perceive blockface street-light brightness conditions in terms of the brightness levels relatively proximate to their own homes. When asked specifically about conditions proximate to their homes, citizens are more accurate still. We also found that citizens who had lived on their block for more than ten years, who had a high school or better education, or who lived on relatively short blocks showed a higher than average degree of accuracy.

As further analysis proceeds, we hope to address the question of which measures can be used most effectively and economically by public officials or public interest groups in measuring the output of these two municipal services. Where we have multiple modes of data collection for the same attribute, such as we have for road roughness, we can begin to answer the question of which mode is most "cost effective" in providing a reliable and valid indicator of that attribute. It would appear, for example, that the observation form developed to measure several attributes of road repair can be used to generate a valid measure of road roughness that is highly associated with both citizen perceptions of roughness and with a mechanical recording of road roughness. Given the considerable economy of administering an observation form as compared to either a survey of residents or the use of the Residential Street Roughness Indicator, one would have to judge the observation form to be the most cost-effective mode of data collection concerning road roughness of those studied.

Notes

1. See Robert A. Bish and Vincent Ostrom, *Understanding Urban Government* (Washington, D.C.: American Enterprise Institute, 1973).

2. Paul A. Samuelson, "The Pure Theory of Public Expenditure," *The Review of Economics and Statistics* 36 (November 1954), pp. 387-89.

3. William J. Baumol, *Welfare Economics and the Theory of the State* (Cambridge: Harvard University Press, 1962); and Mancur Olson, *The Logic of Collective Action* (Cambridge: Harvard University Press, 1965).

4. For a discussion of the loss of information about the large volume of service calls and activity levels resulting from a police department's primary reliance upon the FBI Index Crimes, see Roger B. Parks, *Measurement of Performance in the Public Sector: A Case Study of the Indianapolis Police Department* (Bloomington,

Indiana: Indiana University, Department of Political Science, Workshop in Political Theory and Policy Analysis, 1971). See also Elinor Ostrom, "Institutional Arrangements and the Measurement of Policy Consequences: Applications to Evaluating Police Performance," *Urban Affairs Quarterly* 6 (June 1971), pp. 447-76.

5. See President's Commission on Law Enforcement and Administration of Justice, *The Challenge of Crime in a Free Society* (Washington, D.C.: U.S. Government Printing Office, 1967).

6. This indicator of performance is utilized in Dennis Smith and Elinor Ostrom, "The Effects of Training and Education on Police Attitudes and Performance: A Preliminary Analysis," in Herbert Jacob, ed., *The Potential for Reform of Criminal Justice* (Beverly Hills: Sage Publications, 1975). For a discussion of other measures of police performance see Elinor Ostrom, "On the Meaning and Measurement of Output and Efficiency in the Production of Urban Police Services," *Journal of Criminal Justice* 1 (June 1973), pp. 93-111.

7. Jerome Skolnick, *Justice Without Trial: Law Enforcement in Democratic Society* (New York: John Wiley & Sons, 1967).

8. Ralph S. Abascal, "Municipal Services and Equal Protection: Variations on a Theme by Griffin V. Illinois," *Hastings Law Journal* 20 (May 1969), pp. 1367-91; Dennis R. Anderson, "Toward the Equalization of Municipal Services: Variations on a Theme by Hawkins," *Journal of Urban Law* 50 (November 1972), pp. 177-97; Michael P. Schumaecker, "Equal Protection: The Right of Equal Municipal Services," *Brooklyn Law Review* 37 (Spring 1971), pp. 568-87.

9. See San Antonio Independent School District v. Rodriquez, 41 U.S.L.W. 4407 (1973); Sweatt v. Painter, 339 U.S. 629 (1950); Serrano v. Priest, 96 Cal. Reptr. 601 (Sup. Cr. Cal., 1961); U.S. v. Jefferson County Board of Education, 380 P. 2d. 385 (5th cir., 1967); Hombson v. Hansen, 269 F. Supp. 401 (D.D.D., 1967).

10. James Coleman, "The Concept of Equality of Educational Opportunity," *Harvard Educational Review* 38 (Winter 1968), pp. 7-22.

11. Elinor Ostrom, William H. Baugh, Richard Guarasci, Roger B. Parks, Gordon P. Whitaker, *Community Organization and the Provision of Police Services* (Beverly Hills: Sage Publications,

1973); Elinor Ostrom and Roger B. Parks, "Suburban Police Departments: Too Many and Too Small," in Louis H. Masotti and Jeffrey K. Hadden, eds., *The Urbanization of the Suburbs* (Beverly Hills: Sage Publications, 1973); Samir T. IsHak, *Consumers' Perception of Police Performance, Consolidation vs. Deconcentration. The Case of Grand Rapids, Michigan Metropolitan Area* (Bloomington, Indiana: Indiana University, Department of Political Science, Workshop in Political Theory and Policy Analysis, 1975); Bruce D. Rogers and C. McCurdy Lipsey, "Metropolitan Reform: Citizen Evaluations of Performance in Nashville-Davidson County, Tennessee," *Publius* (Spring 1975).

12. See Andrew J. Boots, Grace Dawson, William Silverman, Harry P. Hatry, *Inequality in Local Government Services: A Case Study of Neighborhood Roads* (Washington, D.C.: The Urban Institute, no date); Donald M. Fisk, Harry P. Hatry, Kathleen Hudak, Kenneth Webb, Robert Fiore, *Measuring the Effectiveness of Local Government Recreation Services* (Washington, D.C.: The Urban Institute, 1972); Richard E. Winnie and Harry P. Hatry, *Measuring the Effectiveness of Local Government Services: Transportation* (Washington, D.C.: The Urban Institute, 1973).

13. See Richard Rich, "The Development of a Technique for the Physical Measurement of Residential Street Lighting" (Bloomington, Indiana: Indiana University, Department of Political Science, Workshop in Political Theory and Policy Analysis, Research Report Number 5).

14. See Richard Rich, "The Development of the Residential Street Roughness Indicator as a Mode of Measurement for the Study of Municipal Services" (Bloomington, Indiana: Indiana University, Department of Political Science, Workshop in Political Theory and Policy Analysis, Research Report Number 6).

15. See Sue Carroll, "An Analysis of the Relationship Between Citizen Perceptions and Unobtrusive Measures of Street Conditions" (Bloomington, Indiana: Indiana University, Department of Political Science, Workshop in Political Theory and Policy Analysis, Research Report Number 10).

16. Ibid.

17. See Vernon Greene, "An Analysis of the Relationship Between Citizen Perceptions and Physical Measures of Street Light-

ing'' (Bloomington, Indiana: Indiana University, Department of Political Science, Workshop in Political Theory and Policy Analysis, Research Report Number 7).

3

The Citizen Component of Policy Evaluation

David A. Caputo

Policy evaluation, as recent attempts to describe and operationalize it illustrate, often proves elusive and fragmentary.[1] Policy analysts, in order to deal with difficult conceptualization and operationalization problems, have developed innovative and often ingenious methods to evaluate the empirical and theoretical implications of public policy decisions. Rather than recounting and critiquing these past attempts, this chapter focuses on the citizen component of policy evaluation and both justifies and suggests a specific methodology that provides for citizen input in policy evaluation.

Justification for the Citizen Component

The citizen, the consumer of policy outputs, has often been ignored or given a minor role in policy evaluation schemes.[a] The usual practice is for the citizen to have a minimal role in the evaluation process and even then the resulting input is often ignored by both policy analysts and public decision makers. While it is easy to become cynical as to why this has happened, a single answer is inadequate and often simplistic, but three general explanatory categories are useful in summarizing why this took place:

In the first place, definitional problems are common. Evaluation by different citizen reference groups will vary considerably. For instance, should only those citizens actually receiving benefits from, or participating in, a program be part of any evaluation effort? Or does every citizen who is part of the political unit deserve to be included in any evaluation process? It is obvious that the very definition of which citizens have a right to participate in policy evaluation decisions will lead to problems involving the scope and

---

[a]This theme is common throughout most of the policy-evaluation literature. Where citizen input is part of the evaluation process, its importance is usually less than that given other components. For an example where this apparently was *not* the case, see *Police Women On Patrol* (Washington, D.C.: The Police Foundation, 1973).

organization of any subsequent evaluation effort. By using the latter definition, the policy analyst may be on more stable ground politically, but the use of that definition will, in most cases, do little to improve his evaluation efforts. Policy scientists have often ignored the definitional problems and this has weakened policy evaluation.

Second, adding a citizen component complicates policy evaluation regardless of who is doing the analysis. After all, so the critics of citizen input contend, human beings tend to be subjective, self-interested, and motivated by concerns that make objective and rational policy evaluation difficult and often misleading.[b] Why should the policy analyst include a citizen component when he already has more objective and "hard" data? This position has two important aspects:

In the first place, policy evaluation is more often done by government agencies or professionals hired by a particular agency. Bureaucracies are reluctant to have evaluation indicate the need for substantial improvement or increased concern for the recipient of their services. Given this, it becomes logical and politically realistic to exclude citizens from policy evaluation and to include objective data based on records such as age, socioeconomic status, and number of users. This information is useful in providing an often impressive display of program effectiveness, but ignores the more subjective nature of direct citizen evaluation.

Related to and actually more bothersome than this practice is the tendency of some policy analysts to dismiss the reactions and feelings of the citizen as either uneducated or irrelevant.[c] In the former case, the analyst dismisses citizen evaluation because the citizen, in the analyst's view, lacks the sophistication and knowledge necessary to complete a "meaningful" evaluation. In the latter case, citizen evaluation is considered irrelevant due to its supposed lack of objectivity or incompatibility with other quantifiable measures.

The third and perhaps the least discussed category is the exclusion of citizen input for political reasons. If political leaders want justification to modify a policy or program, they may be quite unwilling to risk citizen input that would make such modification

---

[b]This response characterized many of the cities with OEO and other community oriented programs.

[c]This is often done explicitly, but also can happen implicitly. For instance, Yehezkel Dror in *Design For Policy Sciences* (New York: American Elsevier, 1971), pp. 89-99, discusses needed research in the policy sciences and tends to elaborate the need to consider and develop more reliable and accurate measures of citizen evaluation.

more difficult.[d] In addition, seeking citizen input on a particular policy, even if support for the policy change is certain, may increase the probability that the same citizens will get involved in the political or evaluative process in the future when their support is not as certain.[e] Thus, the politician has come full circle; he may be reluctant to activate citizen input for he fears the future potential of that input.

A final point needs to be made concerning the third category. Policy evaluation often involves programs or policies affecting groups that have traditionally been less than full partners in the American political process. The nonwhite and poor often have little direct input in any evaluation effort for the reasons already cited. In these cases, lack of input is an extension of their general lack of political strength, a situation that will not be alleviated or remedied until there is concerted political organization at various levels but especially the local level.[f] To ignore this basic fact is to misunderstand the dynamics of not only policy evaluation, but American politics.

If policy evaluation is to become more sophisticated and applicable to more policy areas, the citizen component must be developed fully. I have argued elsewhere that even if objective data show a policy to be highly effective, the perception and ultimate evaluation of the policy by the citizen directly affected by it must be taken into account.[2] If this is not done, policy evaluation runs the grave risk of either ignoring the citizen or perhaps even worse discounting such evaluation efforts including citizen input when they are inconsistent with the more objective measures usually used for evaluation purposes. This raises a major theoretical problem for the policy analyst that is often ignored and overlooked.

What exactly is the goal of program evaluation? Is it to insure maximum efficiency (each dollar spent gets the maximum return) or maximum effectiveness (total program achieves a certain level of

---

[d]This should not be surprising to political scientists, but it is a fact of political life that is often ignored.

[e]Richard L. Cole develops a related point in his research dealing with citizen participation. Richard L. Cole, *Citizen Participation And Urban Public Policy* (Lexington, Mass.: Lexington Books, D.C. Heath and Co., 1974).

[f]In essence, effective and regular citizen input is directly related to access and political power or the potential for that power. The politically disadvantaged may be able to use the evaluation process as a means to increase their overall political strength within a specific geographical or political area.

success) for a particular program? The efficiency versus effectiveness paradox has usually been resolved with greater emphasis on efficiency. The ideal situation would result in both goals being sought and an optimum level obtained for each. If this is done, the citizen component becomes invaluable in helping to achieve both efficiency and effectiveness since citizen perception of the program is as significant as the objective measures used to measure the program's value. While political scientists have utilized the social psychologist's notion of perception, many policy analysts have tended to ignore the importance of citizen perception in refining and applying their evaluation methodologies.[g] To continue to do so will create serious problems and obvious deficiencies in any policy evaluation methodology.

Conceptualizing the Citizen Component

While it is impossible to operationalize the citizen component in this brief chapter, it is possible to point out the major concepts that must characterize any attempt to develop the citizen component. To begin with, there is no "right" or "one" way to conceptualize and subsequently operationalize the citizen component. If there were, evaluation problems would be minimal. In spite of this lack of unity, operationalization of the citizen component should not be dictated solely by the particular policy or program being evaluated. The optimum strategy is to develop a methodology broad enough to incorporate citizen evaluation of widely different policies in order to increase compatibility and to permit individual methodological adaptations to meet the specific needs of the policy or program being evaluated. This middle range approach will provide maximum returns and increases comparability. Such an approach will include the following five variables:

1. *Participation characteristics:* Evaluation efforts must include not only those who actually participated in or benefited from a particular policy, but a thorough description of which individuals or groups did not participate or benefit. In the case of those who did

---

[g]The point needs to be understood fully. An individual's perception of reality may be just as important and even more relevant to policies affecting that reality than objective measures of that reality. Policy analysts need to develop a notion of perceptual reality in any evaluation attempts.

participate or benefit, comprehensive background data is useful and should be obtained whenever possible and whenever such information does not invade the citizen's privacy. Examples of needed information include source of information about the program, reasons for participating, satisfaction levels, and the usual demographic data (age, sex, socioeconomic characteristics) associated with participation. The purpose is to provide the policy analyst with a comprehensive description of who participates and who receives benefits.

Coupled with this is the need to know who does not participate or receive benefits. Much of this information can be surmised from known census or other survey data and can be used to develop a profile of those not affected by the program. While the importance of participant characteristics may appear obvious, they are often overlooked by policy evaluation attempts that assume a particular policy has similar participation rates by all groups affected. In addition, the absence of information about lack of participation limits evaluation.

2. *Program impact:* A thorough and comprehensive set of measures must be developed that considers both intended and unintended program results. Intended results characterize most policy evaluation and result in an emphasis on number of citizens treated, improvement in various objective measures, or an accounting of "successful" cases. The use and improvement of such measures must continue, but measures of unintended program impact must be considered more fully.

Unintended or second order program impact occurs when a policy or program causes changes in other policy or program areas. For instance, a reduction of drug use due to a drug program may have consequences for unemployment or crime rates within the program area. The magnitude and direction of that impact must be understood fully by the policy analyst if the true impact of the program is to be understood and meaningful evaluation completed. Only when the unintended as well as the intended program impacts are understood fully can comprehensive policy evaluation occur.

3. *Future needs:* Too often program evaluation and policy analysis in general fails to consider the future needs of participants in a program or those affected by a policy. For instance, if a particular program has the effect of providing job skills, but the economy does not have jobs available, is the program successful? This aspect of evaluation needs to take into account the future program and policy

needs of the citizens who are being affected by an initial program or policy. Put another way, evaluation of programs dealing with today's problems without anticipating tomorrow's needs may result in effective and efficient programs in the short run, but programs that have little future importance. The policy analyst should consider the future needs for society and the citizens affected by a particular program and how those needs can best be met. Unless this is done, evaluation becomes little more than an historical review of program success or failure and has little applicability in meeting society's future needs.

4. *Resolution of impact and needs conflict*: The least considered dimension of policy analysis (and specifically policy evaluation) is the need to resolve or at least recognize possible discrepancies between variables 2 and 3. For instance, it is possible for a particular policy to achieve its intended impact with few undesirable second order consequences, but still have little relevancy for future needs of the groups involved. If this is the case, the policy will be difficult to justify. A different possibility is that the policy is not gaining its intended results, but may be meeting desired future needs. While this is more difficult to ascertain, it should be explored carefully before a specific program or policy is discarded. Short-range impact should not be the sole criteria for program evaluation.

An excellent example of the need to resolve the conflict between variables 2 and 3 occurred in the evaluation efforts of the various community action agencies associated with efforts to deal with urban poverty. Few met their stated goal of dealing effectively with poverty, but some of them did sensitize community organizers and the poor to the long-range organizational problems and political opposition they face if they were to be successful in mobilizing the poor or even a politically significant segment of that population. The point should be clear: Effective policy evaluation must attempt to both explain and justify differences between variables 2 and 3.

5. The final variable follows from the preceding four and requires that any policy evaluation be dynamic, that is, a particular evaluation be placed in a continuing time perspective and the individual attributes of any one particular evaluation compared with the results of others throughout a finite period. Too often policy evaluation fails to consider the analysis as part of a dynamic social process; the result is static analysis that may provide a useful and valid description at a particular point in time, but that fails to consider

adequately changes over time. Such changes, especially when the citizen component is involved, may be critical to the analysis.

These five variables provide the basis for a variety of policy evaluation models and typologies that would significantly advance the applicability and utility of policy evaluation. Without full consideration of these variables and the impact they may have on one another and the policy process itself, policy evaluation will remain less than optimal and will continue to provide evaluation results reflecting the static rather than dynamic attributes of public policy.

While the complexity and comprehensive nature of the citizen component and the variables necessary for its injection into policy evaluation have been stressed, it is important to point out that the policy analyst need not feel his task is unmanageable or impossible. The policy analyst must develop a greater sensitivity to the subtleties of the citizen component and research strategies to deal productively with them. If this is not done, policy analysis will see little improvement in either its techniques or their applicability to the universe of policy matters. Policy evaluation that gives careful and thoughtful consideration to citizen input has the potential for significant political and social impact. Hopefully policy scientists will achieve the potential policy evaluation promises.

Notes

1. As readers of this volume are well aware, the literature dealing with policy analysis has increased in the last few years. Representative, but not exhaustive, examples of various approaches to description and operationalization of both policy analysis and policy evaluation include: Boyce, David E. and Norman D. Day, *Metropolitan Plan Evaluation Methodology* (Philadelphia: Institute for Environmental Studies, 1969); Campbell, Donald T. and Julian C. Stanley, *Experimental and Quasi-Experimental Designs for Research* (Chicago: Rand McNally, 1969); Dror, Yehezekel, *Design For Policy Analysis* (New York: American Elsevier, 1971); Glennan, Thomas K., Jr., *Evaluating Federal Manpower Programs: Note and Observations* (Santa Monica: Rand Corporation, 1969); Hess, Robert D. and Jane L. Tapp, *An Evaluation of the Effectiveness Of A Community Based Manpower Training Program* (Chicago: University of Chicago, 1967); Jones, Charles O., *An In-*

troduction To The Study Of Public Policy (Belmont, California: Wadsworth, 1970); Lindblom, Charles E., *The Policy-Making Process* (Englewood Cliffs, N.J.: Prentice-Hall, 1968); Muth, Richard, *The Evaluation of Present and Potential Poverty Programs* (Arlington, Va.: Institute for Defense Analysis, 1966); Rivlin, Alice M., *Systematic Thinking For Social Action* (Washington, D.C.: The Brookings Institution, 1971), Sharkansky, Ira, ed., *Policy Analysis in Political Science* (Chicago: Markham, 1970); and Wholey, Joseph S., John W. Scanlon, Hugh G. Duffy, James S. Fukumor, Leone M. Vogt, *Federal Evaluation Policy* (Washington, D.C.: The Urban Institute, 1970).

2. Caputo, David A., "The Evaluation of Urban Public Policy: A Developmental Model and Some Reservations," *Public Administration Review* 33 (March-April 1973), pp. 113-19.

4 Social Indicators and Policy Analysis

Eugene J. Meehan

Men, as Michael Oakeshott wrote most aptly, " sail a boundless and bottomless sea; there is neither harbour for shelter nor floor for anchorage, neither starting place nor appointed destination." But few men have been content to develop a strategy of living bounded by Oakeshott's view of the human situation. History is an almost continuous record of man's unremitting efforts to gain some measure of control over his destiny, to give his life meaning, or at least to gain some measure of advantage over his fellow man, whatever the ultimate meaning of the human journey. The search for ways of anticipating what tomorrow may bring, of shaping the structure of the morrow in foreseeable desired ways, of comparing and evaluating alternative means of conducting the human voyage, is a constant in all eras of history for all manner of men. The quality of the effort has varied enormously: Men have grounded their beliefs in absurdity or even impossibility, rejected the evidence of the senses in favor of the advice of oracles, of those who read auspices in the entrails of chickens, of those with advanced degrees in economics, postulated the destination of the human voyage in absolute and irrefragable terms then killed, sometimes in quite disagreeable ways, those who disagreed. On the other hand, men have at rare times demonstrated a wondrous capacity for determining the details of tomorrow's world and even used that capacity with a degree of wisdom, humanity, and tolerance that is both surprising and a cause for cautious optimism. In human affairs there has been improvement and debilitation. For some the voyage through life has been made longer, safer, more pleasant and satisfying, a closer approximation to the fullness of human potential than ever before; for others time and experience have done little to ameliorate the struggle for a bare existence. The increased human capacity for disrupting the human voyage is called to attention most forcefully by the mushroom cloud and the massive cumulation of pollutants; improvements in man's capacity to produce a better voyage for all the passengers, as in medicine or agriculture, produce less spectacular resonances on the

33

drumheads of the mass media, but their implications for the human future, particularly in the long run, are likely to be as great as the potential for destruction.

The fundamental human problem, today as in the past, is to bring the human enterprise under intellectual control, to harness the human capacity to reason to the service of humanity—even if the outcome is achieved in the pursuit of selfish interests, the collective benefits may be substantial. The vast increase in the human capacity to alter and control the world is almost meaningless unless it is paralleled by a significant expansion in human awareness and understanding of the factors that most contribute to the quality of the journey through time. And both empirical and normative competence must be linked securely to the management of human affairs. Without some institutional arrangement by which the policies men use to direct their individual and collective affairs can be informed by the best knowledge man can generate, the ship to which all of our lives and fortunes are bound is likely to founder and the quest for knowledge becomes a form of self-indulgence. To achieve that synthesis, knowledge must be constructed as the capacity for engineering the human condition in both its empirical and normative dimensions and not as an art form. That, I believe, is the context in which the potential contribution of social indicators to policy analysis or policy making should be examined.

The focus on the potential value of social indicators rather than their present worth is deliberate—and necessary. The so-called social indicator movement surfaced in the United States in the mid-1960s. While it a has attracted a great deal of governmental and scholarly interest and substantial amounts of financial support, in Western Europe as well as the United States, its practical impact has been meagre.[1] A journal has been established (*Social Indicators Research*, edited by Alex C. Michalos) together with a Center for the Coordination of Research on Social Indicators (funded by the Social Science Research Council using National Science Foundation money) that publishes a newsletter periodically. Meetings have been held. And since both the Russell Sage Foundation and the National Science Foundation have provided substantial amounts of resources for social indicators research, studies have been made and the results duly published.[2] Nevertheless, there is little if any evidence to suggest that any agency of government, in the United States at least, has improved its performance one whit as a result of all this activity. Moreover, if the direction of development established during the first decade is continued, the social indicators movement is unlikely to contribute significantly to improved governmental performance in the future and there is a real danger that it will destroy by misuse a potentially valuable concept in policy analysis.[a]

A variety of factors has contributed to the failure in the policy arena, not least the scholastic tradition of knowledge for the sake of knowledge that still dominates the social sciences. Discussions of social indicators tend to vagueness and generality, making it difficult to relate them to concrete human affairs. While they have focused on observables, they rarely make reference to concrete and specific observations, a common practice in social science and the humanities that provides a spurious aura of relevance to the results without creating relevant and useful knowledge. And social indicators research has been grossly overfunded, that is, funded beyond its theoretical capacity to absorb the resources in research whose theoretical and practical relevance has been established; such overfunding has been at least partly responsible for the frequent and often stupid commission of the availability fallacy by those trying to illustrate the applications of their indicators. Most important of all, the conceptual and theoretical underpinning of the inquiry into social indicators has not been elaborated with sufficient accuracy and precision, primarily because those involved in the movement have not really agreed on the purposes, if any, that indicators were expected to serve. Earlier inquiries focused mainly on the need to monitor social change and the effects of social action; indeed, one of the pioneer works in the field originated in NASA's desire to learn the impact of the space program on the wider society.[3] Similar concerns generated Bertram Gross' effort to produce an analog to the system of national accounts developed by American economists as well as the concern with periodic social reporting that characterizes the Department of Health, Education, and Welfare's study

---

[a]In 1971-72 the National Science Foundation provided the University of Michigan with more than one million dollars for social indicators research. Funded programs included the following:

Social change and collective violence in Europe: 1830-1930
Political indicators and political change
A longitudinal study of community in Detroit
American attitudes and values toward violence
Correlates of international war
Electoral behavior and the meaning of politics

Reconciling these titles with a commitment to social indicators research involves a rather serious extension of that unfortunate phrase.

Toward a Social Report.[4] Such efforts overlapped with the activities of a fairly large group in the movement who were seeking social indicators that could be used in policy making and policy evaluation as well as in monitoring social conditions.[b] Finally, the 1970s brought another term, the "quality of life," into currency, in part as a result of growing interest and concern with conditions in the physical environment and their impact on the population.[5]

Unfortunately, these various goals were seldom spelled out very precisely; hence the kinds of instruments and procedures required to attain them could not be articulated—and criticisms of proposed improvements in the indicators could not be tested. Thus, the precise nature of "social change," and the reason for its importance, were not made clear, though it was asserted rather dogmatically by some that improvement in the field of social indicators was absolutely contingent on the development of precise measures of such changes.[6] Again, there is no sustained discussion of the meaning of "policy" by those who sought indicators that would be useful in policy making. While the criticism may seem severe, a search for indicators, taken seriously, implies a commitment to very careful and sophisticated conceptual and theoretical reasoning. Failure to maintain the integrity of the concept, to keep its intention stable and to provide adequate theoretical links between concept and indicator emasculates the enterprise. The concepts needed to take stock of the human condition are very complex variables, analytically equivalent to theories; the value taken by the complex variable is determined by a set of interactions among its constituent elements that must be specifiable in terms of rules of interaction that must be known before the concept can be applied. That total structure will include, logically and empirically, the indicator used to apply it —indicators are *part of* the concepts that they indicate. That is, if health is taken to be a dimension of human life that requires measurement, anyone proposing to use infant mortality rates as an indicator of health must supply the intervening connections, tell us why infant mortality can serve as an indicator of health as defined. That requires the development of a complex variable in which infant mortality rates play an integrated part, are incorporated into the structure.

The failure to distinguish concept from indicator has been responsible for much of the conceptual confusion in the social indi-

[b]Among others, Bertram Gross, Mancur Olson Jr., Daniel Bell, and Albert D. Biderman.

cator movement. Too often, the concept being indicated was simply taken for granted—in effect, concept and indicator were collapsed, as in radical operationalism. Received opinion and common usage are poor guides in such cases. The fact that a particular statistic is gathered regularly and widely used, accepted, or even acted upon, does not make it a good indicator of some significant dimension of human life.[7] Given the current state of social science, skepticism with respect to concepts is a necessity. Social policy making will require us to weigh the relative merits of alternative outcomes defined in terms of sets of very complex variables—and to do so consistently. Proposals for cancer research must be weighed against primary education or the development of sophisticated weapons systems. Hardly any of the concepts in current use in social science (or available in the main stream of the humanities) can be used for systematic evaluation and criticism of policies. Neither the philosophers or the social scientists, nor those concerned with development of social indicators, seem to be developing concepts with the breadth, precision, and generality that social policy requires, though some of the conceptual criticism has been excellent.[8]

In spite of the poor track record of the social indicator movement in the policy field, the idea of developing some kind of scoring system for society, analogous to the set of "vital signs" that physicians use for describing the condition of patients, is intuitively attractive. Such indicators, if they were available, would be extremely valuable. Analytic considerations reinforce the evaluation and suggest both the possibility of developing such indicators and the direction in which the effort should be placed. If we return to the set of basic conditions that must be satisfied if we are to produce reasoned and defensible, hence corrigible and cumulable policies, the meaning of a set of useful social indicators can be rooted in that context. That is, the concepts and indicators required for or useful in policy making should fulfill the functions for which social indicators are sought—provide a way of keeping track of social changes and assessing their effects, focus attention on salient social problems or provide an early warning system for social upheaval. In the process, the utility of the social indicators can be established as well; the procedure tests the assumptions on which the search for social indicators is predicated. In the process, for reasons to be made clear below, both the possibility of and the need for an independent field of study focused on social indicators simply disappears.

The usefulness of validity of the concept of "policy" employed in inquiry depends on a fairly complex set of assumptions relating to the purposes that human knowledge must satisfy, the instruments and processes required, and the limits of the human capacity to generate knowledge in that sense. Usually, such fundamentals are simply taken for granted. In those disciplines where the underlying assumptions are well established (though not necessarily well articulated) and fully incorporated into professional training, that causes no special problems. But in policy analysis, the fundamental assumptions from which inquiry proceeds are not only poorly articulated, they differ greatly from one inquirer to another and the differences are only rarely surfaced let alone brought to resolution. Since criticism is meaningful only within some specified conceptual framework, that basic structure must be articulated if we are to expose the criticism to further criticism and thus open the door to refinement and improvement of the apparatus. Common usage cannot serve as guide because it varies from simply identifying policy with statements of aspirations to treating particular kinds of governmental proclamations as policies. In the present context, the most germane form of common usage treats a policy as a guide to action or choice—in the sense of a prescribed program of medical treatment for a known ailment. Since the quality of guides to action can vary enormously, the meaning of that phrase will have to be constrained; in effect, the conditions must be identified in which policies that are useful, defensible, and corrigible can be created within the limits of known human capacity. The instrument, the policy, must be both possible and worth having, useful for human purposes that are agreed to be worth fulfilling. If that can be done, the instrument is worth pursuing even if the critic argues that it is not an adequate way of conceptualizing or defining policy.

Analytically, every human action involves an actor, an action, and a set of outcomes or consequences. Since actions necessarily produce difference or change in the observed world, the consequences of action are always a world that is somehow different than it would otherwise be. Consequences can therefore be expressed in the general form: Action produced situation S_1 *instead of* situation S_2. Actions are therefore precisely equivalent to choices. Furthermore, failure to act when the capacity to alter the world is present counts as action because the world is different than it might have been had the capacity been exercised. While actions might in principle be criticized by reference to either the actor, the action, or the consequences of action, in practice, criticism must focus on the consequences because an action or actor focus leads to inconsistency. That is, if actions are criticized in terms of the actor, the same action will have to be evaluated differently if performed by different actors with different moral worth even if the consequences are identical. Similarly, criticism focused on the intrinsic properties of actions leads to an identical appraisal of actions whose consequences differ radically. Such anomalies, the result of collapsing criticism of an action with criticism of an actor, are avoided if the two tasks are kept separate; actions are judged by their consequences, actors are judged in terms of the consequences of their actions, but modified in the light of intentions, knowledge, and so on. That focus has the added virtue of allowing the critic to function effectively without knowing either the identity of the actor or his policies or intentions—which is particularly valuable with respect to social affairs and governmental actions.

Actions, then, are attacked or defended by comparing the outcome that followed from the action (the situation the action produced) with the situations that could have been produced by the same actor had he refrained from acting or had he acted in a different way. In effect, criticism requires a cost-benefit analysis of the various options available to a specified actor in a given situation, though neither costs nor benefits need be specified in money terms. In that context, reasoned or corrigible choices are contingent on four primary conditions: First, theories are needed that can project the alternatives available to the actor with accuracy and reliability, for choices are made with respect to the attainable future; second, an agreed set of concepts or variables is required that will identify the normatively significant dimensions of the situation and thus provide the continua for comparing the various available outcomes; third, a priority structure or preference-ordering (value system) must be available or created that will identify the preferred outcome among the available options; fourth, a rule of choice must be created that will apply the priority structure to the case in hand. That rule of choice is the best available candidate for the label *policy*. That is, construed as a guide to action, policy is best defined as the instrument used to apply a priority structure to a particular choice situation. That links the concept into the wider structure that specifies the conditions required for reasoned choice and thus brings into play all of the methodological criteria available for criticism of the results of inquiry.

Since the alternatives from which a choice is made must be real and possible, within the capacity (not legal competence) of a known actor, the need for adequate theories is absolute. Without them, there is nothing to compare, hence no basis for action. A forecast, however accurate, is not an adequate basis for choice because it provides no intervention strategy, no way of acting to bring about the desired outcome. Forecasts require the assumption that observation of one change justifies the expectation that another change will occur. Theories require a further assumption that there is a causal relation between one change and another so that any action that produces one change can be expected to bring about its companion change. Of course, a forecast that estimates the number of persons expected to die in a given geographic location may aid the undertaker in his business but it provides no information that can be used to increase or decrease the number of deaths.

The concepts used to compare the various outcomes that can be achieved by human action will vary with time, culture, and ethical development as well as the particular situation. In the last analysis, however, those concepts must refer to the effects of human action on human objects. For man, there is no viable alternative to treating man as the measure of all things, to what is called radical individualism in ethics. Without human life there would be nothing to criticize, no one to do the criticizing, and no one to be concerned with its quality—the whole enterprise becomes absurd. While social features such as stability or wealth or mobility are convenient to use they are never more than intervening variables in the calculation of the consequences of action. Before they can be used in criticism or policy making, they must be linked securely to specified changes in the conditions of life of specified populations. Actually, radical individualism simplifies the conceptual apparatus needed for criticizing choices. Since any individual can be conceived as a set of variables whose values at any point in time are determined by observation or are predictable by an appropriate theory, the consequences of action can always be specified as a set of changes in the values of the set of variables used to define an individual or population. If the values have not changed, there has been no action. A justification of the action can be provided if reasons can be offered for preferring one set of values for those variables to other achievable sets of values for the same set, including a specification of the assumptions on which those reasons depend. If no reason for preference ordering can be found, the choice is a matter of indifference given the accepted ethic. This procedure eliminates the need for absolute standards for measuring the normative quality of actions of outcomes; all that reasoned choice requires is some reason for preferring one outcome to the others in a set.

The priority structure is a consequence of the solution of particular cases, aggregated and generalized in the same way as scientific theories. In practice, every individual is born into a culture containing a number of priority structures and no one can live very long without one. The problem is to correct and improve, not to build priorities from scratch. Criticism begins *in medias res*; it is neither possible nor necessary to begin with a blank slate. While the total content of the priority structure need not be integrated, that is, derived from some common set of axioms, it must be consistent where priorities intersect or overlap. Tea may be preferred to coffee and ice cream to cookies, for example, without contradiction, and the priority to be assigned to tea and ice cream does not have to be settled until the choice actually appears. But if coffee is preferred to ice cream, then consistency requires that coffee should also be preferred to cookies in the same general situation, other things equal. The priority structure evolves continually as new possibilities are created by knowledge expansion, improved technology, or increased resources. That is the reason why each application of the priority structure should in principle be regarded as a test of both the priorities and the definition of the situation to which the priorities are applied by a particular policy. When the established priority structure does not cover the situation at hand, it must be expanded; if no reason can be found for preferring one outcome to another the action can be treated as an experiment—the choice can be made randomly and the conditions resulting compared with the conditions anticipated from acting differently. Such tentative choices, deliberately opened to sequential modification over time, are very important in complex situations where projections of outcomes are weak and vague and the consequences of action likely to be significant—in governmental actions in new program areas, for example.

The analytic separation of the priority structure and the policy or choice rule is essential to avoid conceptual confusion. Priorities differ from policies in the same way that the desire to minimize disfigurement due to medical treatment differs from prescribing a particular treatment for a particular patient. It allows the critic to change the policy while retaining the priority structure, or to change the priority structure while retaining the policy. Both actions are needed in real life situations. In all cases, the policy must be stated in a way that will *force* a choice in a specified situation; being compatible with one alternative and not the others is insufficient. A law that allows the angler to keep all fish of a particular species if they are more than 18 inches in length enjoins throwing back the fish if it is below that length but says nothing about the angler's decision when the fish is more than 18 inches long. An illustration of the value of separating policy from priorities is found in the child given a choice between two coins of unequal value. If the child prefers a larger to a smaller monetary value, it can nevertheless make use of various policies to make its choices—choose the largest coin, choose the silver coin, and so on. A policy that works well in some situations may break down completely in others. "Choose the largest coin," for example, will provide acceptable results when applied to a choice between quarters and dimes but will break down when applied to the choice between a dime and a nickel—the benefits obtained by the policy, measured in terms of the accepted priority structure, are fully contained in another outcome that carries some surplus. When issues are complex, a considerable number of policies will be required, and maintaining the internal consistency of the structure may be a serious problem. Such terms as "housing policy," for example, are labels for large and complicated sets of choice rules which relate to such particulars as design, construction, rental, maintenance, and so on; they must be unpacked into constituent elements before systematic criticisms can be made.

Construed in this way, policy making is inventory management of a rather special kind and an inventory of state-one conditions, specified in terms of the concepts incorporated into the priority structure, is essential. Since the consequences of choice can always be stated as changes in the human condition induced by human action, policies will serve either to increase or to decrease the differences among specified individuals or groups. The groups will be defined by reference to the same set of priorities. Assessments of significance depend on the same application of the concepts in the priority structure but take into account the level of priority assigned to them. That is, any concept can in principle serve as a normative variable, and in a world without scarcities it would at some point come into play. But in a world where scarcity is unavoidable, there is always a cut-off point, a set of dimensions of the situation that must be disregarded for lack of resources. Something else will have a higher priority. Scarcity is an important simplifier in normative affairs; in very poor societies, most of the basic decisions can be made by reference to the bare essentials for sustaining life, though quite nasty decisions will have to be made if the scarcity is so severe that not all of the life in the society can be sustained, whatever the system of distribution adopted. At the other end of the continuum, wealthy societies, where the capacity is great, encounter more difficult normative problems than do poor societies—and distribution procedures are correspondingly more important.

What role can "social indicators" play in the kind of policy-making enterprise sketched so briefly above? In the empirical phase of policy making, the development of the theoretical capacity to project the consequences of action accurately and reliably, indicators will certainly be needed for the various concepts employed, but that is not the sense in which the term "social indicators" is normally used. And on the normative side of the program, the set of concepts and indicators used in the priority structure is clearly the heart of the enterprise. The concepts will refer to the attributes of individuals accepted as normatively significant by the actor or critic. They will be used to structure the outcomes from which choices are made or alternatively to produce an inventory of state-one conditions that can serve as a basis for policy evaluation. Such concepts will obviously require indicators. But again that is not the meaning normally intended by the term "social indicator."

In current usage, the term "social indicators" tends to imply changes in the features of society that provide some indication of the condition of the parts, or conditions of the aggregate that have significant implications for the conditions of the parts—defined in normative terms. Such concepts (or indicators) would play the same role in social inquiry that "vital signs" play in medicine. But those concepts are clearly contingent upon or derivative from the set of concepts employed in the priority structure and not independently generated. That is, a clear theoretical connection is needed between the concept used as a social indicator (infant mortality, social cohesiveness, etc.) and specific values or changes in values in the set of normative concepts that appear in the priority structure. If there is no connection, there is no way to attach significance to changes in the values of the variables used as indicators—significance is a function of the normative variables in the priority structure. Given the assumption of radical individualism, no social feature has intrinsic importance. Of course, the fact that social indicators are contingent need not make them trivial. One major function of social science is to demonstrate the relation between structural and other changes in the features of society and the conditions of life of specified features of the population, measured in terms of a set of normative variables. Most policies function by altering social structure or social features, and in the absence of adequate theoretical constructions or linkages, can be no more than "first steps in the right direction" predicated in faith rather than reason. Given the analytic priority of the normative variables in the priority structure, the search for social indicators cannot be an independent form of inquiry though it could contribute substantially to the development and improvement of the conceptual apparatus used for criticism and evaluation of choice.

The same reasoning applies when social indicators are construed as devices for providing an early warning system for society as a whole. While a simple predictor of catastrophe would be useful, its usefulness is contingent upon the state of knowledge available externally and not its intrinsic merits—the predictor is contingent on some prior conception of the nature of catastrophe. In effect, there can be no vital signs without a prior science of medicine, no set of symptoms without an established disease. And since every event in society can in principle be conceptualized in an infinite number of different ways, the need for some prior assessment of significance, framed in terms of known normative variables, cannot be avoided simply by "monitoring social change." In the absence of a basis for making a selection, the task is unmanageable and pointless.

In sum, the notion that something called "social indicators" can have an independent existence, can serve as an object of inquiry apart from an ongoing social science, is very badly mistaken. The only possible way to produce social indicators is to advance the social sciences in ways that are relevant for making policy. That implies a commitment to purposeful action, a construction of social science along clinical lines, which is considerably at odds with the approach to inquiry current within the social indicators movement—and within social science generally. To give but one example, no one concerned with policy analysis would be content to describe or examine social change; policy analysis requires knowledge of *the relation between two or more changes* in the environment. It follows that the practice of replicating "baseline studies" advocated by Otis D. Duncan and others has virtually no value for the policy maker. If the original research focused on the relation among changes in the values of a specified set of variables, then replication with a new population would be virtually impossible because of the changes in external factors that could not be identified or controlled. If the original research did not focus on the relation among changes, no amount of replication could extract that information from the environment. Moreover, if the original design focused on the relations among changes, it would have to be applied at least twice to produce the evidence from which the relation could be inferred and examined—otherwise the assumptions on which such assessments are based cannot be satisfied. In that case, the time interval of more than 20 years that appears in Duncan's 1971 study of Detroit could not possibly produce a valid time series, a useful base for studying the relation among changes. Similar criticisms can be leveled against most other research programs undertaken in the social indicator movement, though space limits do not permit them here. Perhaps the most that can be said for the social indicator movement is that it provides an opportunity for social scientists to discover, or perhaps rediscover, the defining parameters of an adequate social science, though it cannot guarantee that this will happen. Given the present state of the social sciences, that may be a significant value. But in the wider context of the need for adequate policy making capacity, it is hardly an adequate justification of the resource expenditures involved.

Notes

1. For a good introductory survey of the movement see: Robert Parke and Eleanor B. Sheldon, *Social Indicators One Year Later; an Overview*, Social Science Research Council, Washington, D.C., mimeographed (Washington, D.C.: Social Science Research Council, no date); Kenneth C. Land, *Social Indicator Models, An Overview*, mimeographed (Washington, D.C.: Russell Sage Foundation, no date); Eleanor B. Sheldon and Howard E. Freeman, *Notes*

on Social Indicators: Promises and Potential, mimeographed
(Washington, D.C.: Russell Sage Foundation, no date); Daniel Bell,
"The Idea of A Social Report," and Mancur Olson Jr., "The Plan
and Purpose of a Social Report," both in *The Public Interest,* Spring
1969; Helmut Klages, "Assessment of an Attempt at a System of
Social Indicators," *Policy Sciences* 4 (1973), pp. 249-61; Bertram
Gross, ed., *Social Goals and Indicators for American Society, The
Annals* (May-Sept. 1967); *Toward a Social Report,* (Washington,
D.C.: Department of Health, Education and Welfare, 1969); Eleanor
B. Sheldon and Wilbert E. Moore, *Indicators of Social Change,*
(Washington D.C.: Russell Sage Foundation, 1968); Angus Camp-
bell and Philip E. Converse, *The Human Meaning of Social Change,*
(Washington, D.C.: Russell Sage Foundation, 1972).

2. Leslie D. Wilcox et al., eds., *Social Indicators and Social
Monitoring: An Annotated Bibliography,* (San Francisco, Calif.:
Jossey-Bass, 1972).

3. Earl P. Stevenson, "Foreword," in Raymond Bauer, ed.,
Social Indicators (Cambridge, Mass.: MIT Press, 1966).

4. See Land, *Social Indicators*; and Mancur Olson Jr., "An
Analysic Framework for Social Reporting and Policy Analysis,"
The Annals, March 1970, pp. 112-26.

5. For a good illustration of the conceptual confusion in this
phase of the indicators movement, see *The Quality of Life Concept:
A Potential Tool for Decision Makers* (Washington, D.C.: Environmental Protection Agency, 1973).

6. Attributed to O.D. Duncan by Parke and Sheldon, *Social
Indicators,* p. 3.

7. For some truly appalling examples of the availability fallacy in
the social indicators movement, see Martin V. Jones and Michael J.
Flax, *The Quality of Life in Metropolitan Washington, D.C.,*
(Washington, D.C.: The Urban Institute, 1970); Michael J. Flax, *A
Study in Comparative Urban Indicators* (Washington, D.C.: The
Urban Institute, 1972); *Social Indicators: 1973,* (Washington, D.C.:
Office of Management and Budget); or *Social Reporting in
Michigan: Problems and Issues,* (State of Michigan: Office of Plan-
ning Coordination, 1970).

8. For example, see Albert D. Biderman, "Social Indicators and
Goals," in Raymond A. Bauer, *Social Indicators,* pp. 68-153 for a
very good treatment of crime statistics.

**Part III
Design**

Introduction to Part III

In general terms, the design of a research project serves as a blue-print for the overall research effort. It spells out how the researcher organized the various aspects of the research problem for purposes of data collection and analysis, the objective being the maximization of internal and external validity within the realistic contraints of the research setting. The chapters in Part III represent a variety of design perspectives applicable to several types of policy analysis problems. Chapter 5 by Virginia Gray argues for a better fit between the analytical model and the theoretical model contained in a study, and points out the need to replace the cross-sectional design with a longitudinal design in those studies analyzing public policy as a process that changes over time. Chapter 6 by Donald S. Van Meter and Herbert B. Asher continues the emphasis upon the need to tie theory and method together within a policy study, and suggests a causal approach toward theory development and data analysis in policy analysis. In particular, the authors discuss the utility of two promising causal modeling approaches, recursive and nonrecursive path estimation techniques. Chapter 7 by E. Terrence Jones addres-ses a neglected area of policy impact analysis, the impact of every-day, incremental changes in policy actions. Using a variant of the nonequivalent control group design as the suggested approach, Jones also points out some of the measurement issues relevant to the measurement of incremental impacts, such as alternative ways of measuring "change" in government spending and manpower alloca-tion. Chapter 8 by Stuart Nagel offers a very promising perspective for future policy analysis. Nagel draws heavily from the operations research literature in suggesting the use of optimizing techniques for locating the best mix of public policies under the ever present constraint of search resources. The discussion is tied into a cost-benefit framework, a topic to be discussed in detail in Chapter 13 by Ronald W. Johnson and John M. Pierce. Chapter 9 by Frank P. Scioli, Jr. and Thomas J. Cook discusses the application of experi-mental design to the assessment of policy impacts. After noting the pros and cons of the experimental approach, the authors offer a design alternative that is applicable under settings favoring both randomized experiments and nonexperimental evaluations of policy impacts. While the selections included in this part do not exhaust the potential design alternatives, they do offer promise of utility under a diversity of policy analysis settings.

5

The Use of Time Series Analysis in the Study of Public Policy

Virginia Gray

The purpose of this chapter is to demonstrate the appropriateness of time series regression applied to the policy process. We begin by arguing its theoretical value, then discuss the few extant examples of such research, and end with the technical problems involved.

Theory

Most comparative studies of policy, especially those at the subnational level, have been cross-sectional in design, that is, the unit of analysis is the governmental system, such as a state, at a single point in time or at repeated points in time.[1] From these static analyses conclusions are sometimes drawn as to how policies can be changed over time. For example, Thomas Dye concluded that his findings from cross-sectional correlations in the early 1960s

warn us not to be optimistic about the policy changes which can be expected from reapportionment, from the growth of two-party government in the South, or from an increase in Negro voter participation.

Economic growth rather than party competition will be the most significant factor in improvements in state education, welfare, highways, and tax programs. Negroes . . . will find that economic development will define what they can provide in the way of public services as it has defined it for white policy-makers.[a]

One might have some confidence that these cross-sectional re-

The author is indebted to W. Phillips Shively, University of Minnesota, for detecting at least one error in an earlier draft of this chapter.

[a]Thomas R. Dye, *Politics, Economics and the Public* (Chicago: Rand McNally and Company, 1966), p. 301. The fundamental question is also often posed in developmental terms as in Dawson, pp. 205-6:

Do relationships between factors such as urbanization and political participation persist through different time periods, or are they related only for some particular historical period? How are changes in levels of economic development related to changes in political composition? Or, more specifically, what impact is increasing industrialization likely to have upon the historical one-party domination in the Southern states?

51

sults are theoretically sound if they are replicated time after time or if the same variables that have high explanatory power for levels of expenditures also explain change in levels of expenditures. Such is not the case, however. Both Frederick Hartwig and Ira Sharkansky have found discrepancies in explaining levels and change; Richard J. Hofferbert has found discrepancies in repeated cross sections.[2] Furthermore, Raymond Boudon has shown that the "cross-sectional illusion" has been responsible for the common impression that cultural inequality is a major determinant of inequality in educational opportunity.[3]

It has been demonstrated by Hayward R. Alker, Jr., according to the covariance theorem, that mathematically there is no reason to expect the total correlation, the cross-sectional correlation, or the time series correlation to be equal.[4] The covariance theorem is: $C_{x,y} = WC_{x,y} + BC_{x,y}$ or total covariance equals within covariance plus between covariance. The between term averages the covariance of the means for a year (or for a system) on X and Y about their universal means; the within term is the average (weighted) of covariances for each year (or system). However, as documented above, the cross-sectional fallacy is frequently found in the substantive literature where usually the choice of a cross-sectional research design is one of convenience and limited resources.

The fundamental distinction is that policy making is a process; it occurs over time within a governmental system such as a state. It does not occur across states; hence, the cross-sectional regression or correlational analysis does not reflect the process from which our data are gathered. On theoretical grounds (whether the theory is the usual application of David Easton's systems theory or not) the focus should be on explaining differences across time.[b] A time series regression approach is the more appropriate technique because the unit of analysis is the system, such as a state, at time $t, t - 1, t - 2$, etc.

It is important to note the different substantive interpretation attached to the regression coefficient, b, according to whether the model is cross-sectional or overtime. In the cross-sectional case $b = (P_i - P_j)/(X_i - X_j)$ where i and j are systems, P is the dependent

[b]A recent review of the policy analysis literature asserts that change is both methodologically and substantively critical for any theory of policy and that all attempts (either at the state or nation level) at comparison rely upon implicit models of policy change. See: Marsha Chandler, William Chandler, and David Vogler, "Policy Analysis and the Search for Theory," *American Politics Quarterly* 2 (January 1974), pp. 107-18.

policy variable, and X is the independent variable such as competition. Here b is estimated from data on all systems in a single year. Thus, states are similar (or different) to the extent they conform to the cross-state pattern (or deviate from the cross-state pattern). In the time series case $b = (P_t - P_{t-1})/(X_t - X_{t-1})$ where t and $t - 1$ are years and X and P are as defined above. Here b is estimated from time series data from each system and is defined in terms of differences through time for a single system. In this form states are similar to the extent that the same processes operate in each of them individually and states are different in the parameters that govern the operation of the processes in each state.[c]

Examples of Time Series Analysis

The first place to start is with Ronald D. Brunner's and Klaus Liepelt's article "Data Analysis, Process Analysis, and System Change," which offers a convincing argument at the cross-national level for shifting to a time series design.[5] Their two studies (of a model from macroeconomics and of the NPD in the Federal Republic of Germany) show that traditional conventions of data analysis are fallacious under reasonably general conditions. Also at the cross-national level is Peters' "Economic and Political Effects on the Development of Social Expenditures in France, Sweden and the United Kingdom."[6] His substantive results are that both economic growth variables and political variables are needed to explain expenditures for social services in five functional areas. He tackles the problem of autocorrelation by adding more variables (in the case of France and the United Kingdom) and (in the case of Sweden) dividing the total time period into two smaller periods around a shift point he notices in the residuals.

At the subnational level one might consult my "Time Series Analysis of State Spending" in which models of the state policy process are evaluated cross-sectionally and over time.[7] There are several interesting reversals from the usual cross-sectional findings:

[c]Ronald D. Brunner and Garry D. Brewer, *Organized Complexity* (New York: Free Press, 1971), pp. 4-7, develop this interpretation for cross-national development theories. From an entirely different perspective Rose has recently argued that the major task of state policy analysis *should be* to explain the similarities among state policies: Douglas D. Rose, "National and Local Forces in State Politics: The Implications of Multi-Level Policy Analysis," *American Political Science Review* 67 (December 1973), p. 1166.

(1) The correlation of competition and turnout within each state is generally much lower than cross-sectionally; (2) the relationship of the measure, welfare share, and per capita personal income is negative over time but positive in cross-sectional data; (3) the relationship of the measure, education effort, and per capita personal income is positive over time but negative in cross-sectional data. These results are from time series regression equations that did not exhibit autocorrelation and whose F-statistics were significant and from cross-sectional regression equations with no multicollinearity and significant F-statistics.

There are many examples one can cite from the economics literature where relationships reverse according to the type of design: The relationship of income to birth rate is negative within household cross sections while the relationship of income to birth rate is positive within business-cycle time series. Similarly, over the business cycle the suicide rate is negatively correlated with the variables income and employment; cross sections show the relationship between family income and suicide rate to be positive.[8] Perhaps for this reason the statistical theory underlying time series regression analysis has been most fully worked out in econometrics; here one can find discussions of the problem of autocorrelation, tests for its presence, and a few solutions for eliminating it.

Problems in Analysis

One reason that time series regression is rarely employed in political science is that a significant problem often crops up—autocorrelation. Consider the following regression equations:

$$Y_t = a + bX_t + e_t \tag{5.1}$$

$$Y_{t-1} = a + bX_{t-1} + e_{t-1} \tag{5.2}$$

which are rendered complex by the subscripts t indicating time, instead of the usual i, indicating a state or other unit. Autocorrelation exists when e_t is correlated, positively or negatively, with e_{t-1}, e_{t-2}, etc. We suspect the errors may be correlated because whatever factors produce the disturbance, e, in one year are likely to carry over into the following year. Jan Kmenta compares autoregression of the disturbances with the effect of tapping a musical string: The sound is loudest at the time of impact but lingers on for awhile.[9] The shorter the time between tapping the strings, the more likely it is that the preceding sound can still be heard. Thus, autocorrelation is more likely in monthly or quarterly data than in annual data.

The reason the correlation of the error terms presents a problem is because one of the assumptions of ordinary least squares (OLS) is no longer met, namely, that disturbance terms are uncorrelated. The estimates of parameters a and b are still unbiased and consistent, but OLS no longer gives efficient estimators, that is, the sampling interval around each estimate is large. Thus, it is difficult to test hypotheses because the R^2 and the t and F statistic tend to be exaggerated.[10]

There are several tests for the presence of serial correlation. One can produce the fitted residuals $\hat{e}_t$ from equation (5.1) and then apply OLS to the equation:

$$\hat{e}_t = \underline{p}\hat{e}_{t-1} + u_t \tag{5.3}$$

The error term u_t now meets OLS assumptions because all the serial correlation is caught by $\underline{p}$. If $\underline{p} = 0$, there is little serial correlation. The most common statistic used to test for autocorrelation, Durbin and Watson's $\underline{d}$, is just an equivalent test for the hypothesis that $\underline{p} = 0$. The values of $\underline{d}$, found in any standard statistical reference, vary with the number of observations and the number of regressors. One shortcoming of $\underline{d}$ is an inconclusive region where one cannot reject the hypothesis that $\underline{p} = 0$ nor accept an alternative hypothesis. Also $\underline{d}$ is not appropriate where one of the regressors is a lagged value of the dependent variable.

A simple but less precise way one can test the residuals for the presence of autocorrelation is by graphing them. If their frequency distribution appears to be bell-shaped (normal), serial correlation is not present. If plotting the residuals on the vertical axis against time on the horizontal axis produces a definite trend, serial correlation is indicated. If fairly smooth long waves show up in the graph, positive serial correlation is indicated; persistent alternations between negative and positive values indicates negative serial correlation.[11]

If one cannot reject the hypothesis of no autocorrelation by any of these procedures, then proceed by OLS. If one can reject the hypothesis of no autocorrelation one must consider using techniques other than OLS. Practical solutions are discussed below; there are many theoretical solutions to be found in the econometrics literature which are impractical in the sense that they require knowledge of $\underline{p}$.

One can choose among several iterative procedures.[12] The Crane-Orcutt procedure is: From equation (5.3) obtain an estimate of p, $\hat{p}$, and construct new variables $(Y_t - \hat{p}Y_{t-1})$ and $(X_t - \hat{p}X_{t-1})$. Use OLS on the equation:

$$(Y_t - \hat{p}Y_{t-1}) = a(1 - \hat{p}) + b(X_t - \hat{p}X_{t-1}) + u_t \qquad (5.4)$$

Get the second round residuals and use them to obtain a new estimate of p, $\hat{p}$; repeat the procedure until the estimates converge.

Durbin's iterative method is: Multiply equation (5.2) by p and subtract the result from equation (5.1) to get:

$$Y_t - pY_{t-1} = a(1 - p) + b(X_t - pX_{t-1}) + (e - pe_{t-1}) \quad (5.5)$$

By equation (5.3) $e_t - pe_{t-1} = u_t$, so we can write

$$Y_t - pY_{t-1} = a(1 - p) + b(X_t - pX_{t-1}) + u_t \qquad (5.6)$$

By rearrangement into the regression equation

$$Y_t = a(1 - p) + pY_{t-1} + bX_t - bpX_{t-1} + u_t \qquad (5.7)$$

$\hat{p}$ can be estimated by OLS. Then use $\hat{p}$ to construct new variables as in equation (5.6) and estimate again as in equation (5.7).

A simpler method, if one can assume $p = 1$, is the method of first differences. Substitute for p and rearrange equation (5.3) so that:

$$e_t - 1e_{t-1} = u_t \qquad (5.8)$$

Recall that u_t meets OLS assumptions. Subtracting equation (5.2) from equation (5.1) yields an equation in the form of first differences:

$$\Delta Y_t = b\Delta X_t + u_t \qquad (5.9)$$

Note that the intercept now drops out of the equation. The estimate of the intercept, if significantly different from 0, can then be interpreted as a linear time trend, that is, it tells how much the variable being explained changes every time period.[13]

The use of first differences is not recommended unless p is believed to be close to 1. In the field of policy analysis, however, the belief that the true value of p is close to unity is reasonable if you examine closely the implications of that assumption. According to Carl F. Christ, the assumption that $p = 1$

means that when a shift occurs in a particular year, it stays forever, moving the curve or surface to a new position, from which the next year's shift is received. There is no average position of the curve or surface, for it can be pushed back or forth quite a distance if several successive shifts should all come in the same direction.[d]

Most studies of budgeting, in particular, and policy making, in general, at the national level and at the state level demonstrate that the decision revolves about increases or decreases to last year's base.[14] Once a new base is achieved it remains until the next year's increment is received. Thus, the crucial assumption in order to use first differences, that $\underline{p} = 1$, may be met in the type of process we typically study.

Conclusion

The appropriateness of a longitudinal design, rather than the typical cross-sectional design, has been argued because the analytic model is isomorphic with the theoretic model, that is, time series regression focuses on a process occurring over time. Results from the few studies employing this research design vary a good deal from those conducted on cross-sectional data. The major stumbling block, autocorrelation, is explained, as well as its solutions. It is suggested that the method of first differences may be suitable for most policy analysis.

Notes

1. Richard E. Dawson, "Social Development, Party Competition, and Policy," in *The American Party System*, William Nisbet Chambers and Walter Dean Burnham, eds. (New York: Oxford University Press, 1967); Richard I. Hofferbert, "Socioeconomic Dimensions of the American States: 1890-1960," *Midwest Journal of Political Science* 12 (August 1968), pp. 401-18; Ira Sharkansky, *Spending in the American States* (Chicago: Rand McNally and Company, 1968); Richard E. Dawson and Virginia Gray, "State Welfare Policies," in *Politics in the American States*, 2nd ed., Herbert Jacob and Kenneth N. Vines, eds. (Boston: Little, Brown and Company, 1971).

[d]Ibid. p. 484, However, the year-to-year change (ΔY_i) must fluctuate randomly about zero, that is, decrements as well as increments must be theoretically possible.

2. Sharkansky, *Spending in the American States*; Frederick Hartwig, "Determinants of Rates of Change: The Case of Combined State and Local Expenditures Per Pupil Between 1940 and 1960," paper presented at the Annual Meeting of the Midwest Political Science Association, Chicago, Illinois, 1973; Hofferbert, "Socioeconomic Dimensions."

3. Raymond Boudon, *Education, Opportunity, and Social Inequality* (New York: John Wiley & Sons, 1974), pp. 111, 195.

4. Hayward R. Alker, Jr., *Mathematics and Politics* (London: Macmillan, 1965), p. 100, or Alker, "A Typology of Ecological Fallacies," in *Quantitative Ecological Analysis in the Social Sciences*, Mattei Dogan and Stein Rokkan eds. (Cambridge: M.I.T. Press, 1969), p. 76, where a more complex version of the theorem is given: $C_{x,y} = WC_{x,y} + BC_{x,y} + TC_{x,y}$ where TC is the trend covariance. This equation decomposes the covariance into three components: temporally averaged within- and between-group (state) terms and an overtime or trend component.

5. Ronald D. Brunner and Klaus Liepelt, "Data Analysis, Process Analysis, and System Change," *Midwest Journal of Political Science* 16 (November 1972), pp. 538-69. Among the more data-oriented articles at the national level is Bruce M. Russett, "Some Decisions in the Regression Analysis of Time-Series Data," *Mathematical Applications in Political Science*, James F. Herndon and Joseph L. Bernd, eds. (Charlottesville: University of Virginia Press, 1971), vol. 5. Russett finds autocorrelation in his variables, defense spending and GNP, and then he unfortunately chooses to ignore the problem in the analysis.

6. B. Guy Peters, "Economic and Political Effects on the Development of Social Expenditures in France, Sweden and the United Kingdom," *Midwest Journal of Political Science* 16 (May 1972), pp. 225-38.

7. Virginia Gray, "Time Series Analysis of State Spending," paper presented at the Annual Meeting of the Midwest Political Science Association, Chicago, Illinois, 1973.

8. For a discussion of these examples and of the problem in general, see: Dennis J. Aigner and Julian L. Simon, "A Specification Bias Interpretation of Cross-Section vs. Time Series Parameter Estimates," *Western Economic Journal* 8 (January 1970), pp. 149-51.

9. Jan Kmenta, *Elements of Econometrics* (New York: Macmillan Co., 1971), p. 270.

10. Douglas A. Hibbs, Jr., "Problems of Statistical Estimation and Causal Inference in Time Series Regression Models," in *Sociological Methodology 1973-1974*, H. L. Costner, ed. (San Francisco: Jossey-Bass, 1974), p. 257. Other standard references are J. Johnston, *Econometric Methods*, 2nd ed. (New York: McGraw-Hill, 1972), chap. 8; and Ronald J. Wonnacott and Thomas H. Wonnacott, *Econometrics* (New York: John Wiley & Sons, 1970), chap. 6.

11. Carl F. Christ, *Econometric Models and Methods* (New York: John Wiley & Sons, 1966), pp. 521-22.

12. Explained in Kmenta, *Elements of Econometrics*, pp. 288-89.

13. Christ, *Econometric Models and Methods*, p. 485.

14. Ira Sharkansky, "Agency Requests, Gubernatorial Support and Budget Success in State Legislatures," *American Political Science Review* 62 (December 1968), pp. 1220-31; Otto A. Davis, M.A.H. Dempster, and Aaron Wildavsky, "A Theory of the Budgetary Process," *American Political Science Review* 60 (September 1968), pp. 529-47; for a "revisionist" explanation of the budgetary process, see John A. Wanat, "Bases of Budgetary Incrementalism," *American Political Science Review* 68 (September 1974), pp. 1221-28.

6

Causal Perspectives on Policy Analysis

Donald S. Van Meter and Herbert B. Asher

Some of the central issues raised in the field of policy analysis can be described accurately as questions of cause and effect. For example, in the comparative state policy literature, the investigation of the determinants of public policy is basically a concern with the socioeconomic and political causal antecedents of policy decisions. Similarly, impact and evaluation studies raise causal questions about the effects of policy decisions. While causal themes are implicit in these research areas, often the theorizing process is not explicitly causal nor do the methodologies employed facilitate causal analysis. Hence, we will argue in this chapter for a more causal approach to theorizing and to data analysis.

Causal Theorizing

It may be the case that the use of causal data analysis techniques will be difficult or even impossible: Certain assumptions may not be met, data may be unavailable, and equation systems may be unidentified. Even in such situations, a causal approach to theorizing is valuable for its heuristic value. Thinking causally about a problem and constructing an arrow diagram that reflects causal processes may often facilitate the clearer statement of hypotheses and the generation of additional insights into the topic at hand. The heuristic value of causal thinking and path diagrams is demonstrated by the following example.

Consider the case of the policy analyst whose task is to advise a decision maker as to how student performance on various standardized tests might be improved. (The reader should bear in mind that the construction of reliable and valid indicators is not our prime concern here, although this is certainly a must if we are to have any confidence in our analysis.) Assume that the decision maker has control over one basic variable: the amount of money to be spent on education. Such a variable might be labeled a manipulable since its

61

level and utilization can be varied by the conscious decision of actors, within certain limits imposed by various external constraints. But rather than simply hypothesize that increased expenditures for education will improve student performance, an assertion contradicted by several studies, the policy analyst might ask the more causally relevant question: How is it that increased expenditures for education might translate into better student performance? That is, what are the ways in which increased expenditures actually produce improved student performance?

The policy analyst might well recognize that options are available as to how additional moneys might best be allocated to improve student performance. For example, should money be channeled into hiring more teachers so as to lower the pupil/teacher ratio, into attracting better teachers, or into improving facilities and developing (or expanding) innovative programs? What might be the optimal mix of funding for these three options? Figure 6-1 shows how we might represent the situation at this stage.

But there are additional variables that impinge upon student performance that are not as directly under the control of the decision maker. These might include the supportiveness of the family environment toward educational achievement, the student's abilities, and the student's affect toward the educational system. In addition, there might be interrelationships among the manipulable and non-manipulable variables. For example, perhaps more and better teachers, facilities, and programs will influence the student's affect toward education. Hence, the policy analyst might come up with the more complete model depicted in Figure 6-2.

Note how the model not only specifies the relationships between the independent variables and the ultimate dependent variable of interest (student performance), but also makes explicit the relationships among the prior variables. Each linkage included implicitly represents an hypothesis that would be tested by estimating the magnitude of the relationship. While actual estimation of the linkages may or may not be possible, depending upon whether satisfactory indicators can be constructed, appropriate data collected, and the like, the point to be made here is that the kind of causal thinking illustrated by the example has greater promise for elucidating better the processes whereby policy decisions are made—and consequences are determined—than simply correlating independent and dependent variables in a relatively unthinking fashion.

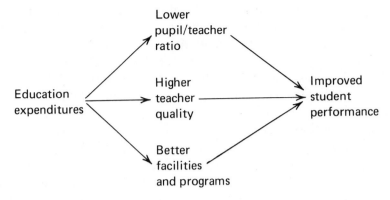

Figure 6-1. Partial Model of Student Performance

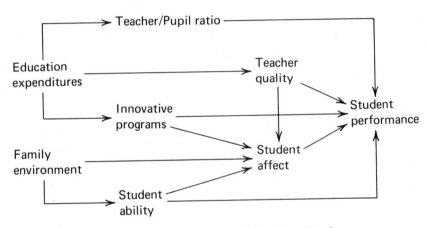

Figure 6-2. Complete Model of Student Performance

The discussion of manipulable variables has implications for the goals of research, the type of statements that one makes, and the kinds of variables that one employs in the actual data analysis. For example, in the comparative state policy literature, the use of factor or composite variables is not uncommon.[1] Such variables are constructed by factor analyzing a set of indicators of some underlying construct (e.g., socioeconomic development), thus creating a factor-variable composed of a weighted combination of the input indicators. Such a variable might then be used in correlation and regression analysis. This procedure might be satisfactory if one is mainly interested in prediction (perhaps as measured by the size of R^2s) and is less concerned about delineating underlying causal processes. But if one wants to make causal statements such as a unit of change in X produces a certain change in Y, what does it mean to talk about a unit change in a socioeconomic factor variable? What components of the factor variables are actually producing the change in the dependent variable? Single item indicators, while perhaps having lower predictive power, are conceptually clearer and lend themselves to more meaningful causal interpretations.

Single item indicators are also superior if one's research is to serve as a productive guide to action for policy makers. Factor variables are essentially nonmanipulable, although their individual components may very well be. For instance, whereas conscious decisions can lead to changes in the salaries of legislators, the availability of staff services, and the number of days the legislature is in session each year, it is difficult to conceive of actors manipulating a factor labeled "legislative professionalism."[2] Hence, our research would have greater relevance for decision makers if we choose for our analysis the best single manipulable variables.

There are many situations, however, in which we do want to employ multiple indicators.[3] In particular, there are numerous areas in policy analysis where we have given an apparently straightforward label to a concept without having thought through its various aspects, thereby relying too heavily on one kind of measurement operation. For example, Elinor Ostrom urges that the outputs of public agencies be measured by multiple indicators.[4] She argues quite cogently that policy outputs have been conceptualized too narrowly and that too great a reliance has been placed on such monetary output measures as total expenditures or per capita expenditures for some public program. She advocates that other modes of data collection be used to generate additional indicators such as citizen perceptions and evaluations of service levels. What we might aim for are multiple indicators of monetary outputs and multiple measures of citizen evaluations.

Causal Data Analysis

Greater attention should also be given to causal data analysis (i.e, causal modeling). A number of techniques can be classified under the heading of causal modeling: these include Simon-Blalock arrow testing, recursive path estimation, and nonrecursive path estimation, which often involves fairly complex econometric estimation techniques.[5] The Simon-Blalock procedure is highly unsatisfactory for it requires a tremendous investment in often unrealistic and restrictive assumptions and yields only weak results—whether or not a linkage belongs in a model without any information as to the magnitude of that linkage. Recursive path estimation, which requires a similar set of assumptions to the Simon-Blalock technique, does yield estimates of the magnitude of the linkages between variables. This allows one to make statements about how a change in one variable affects another variable and enables one to talk about direct and indirect effects of one variable upon another. Nonrecursive path estimation allows one to handle reciprocal relationships, thereby yielding a better representation of real world processes.

Recursive Path Estimation

Recursive path estimation is probably the causal technique that is most compatible with the existing statistical skills of policy analysts and that has widespread applicability. In order to perform recursive path estimation, certain assumptions must be met; these include the standard ones associated with the use of multiple regression.[6] Hence, if these assumptions are met, then the estimation does not require the acquisition of new, sophisticated analysis techniques. The standard list of assumptions in the recursive case includes: (1) linear and additive relationships; (2) interval level data; (3) disturbance terms uncorrelated with the explanatory (predictor or independent) variables in the equations in which they appear; and (4) no confounding unmeasured variables.

To clarify these last assumptions, consider the simple, three variable model shown in Figure 6-3 (which has been extracted from our more complete model of student performance). X_1, X_2, and X_3 are all measured variables, while R_u and R_v are disturbance terms representing those variables not formally included in the model that influence the endogenous variables (i.e., those variables influenced by other measured variables). p_{21}, p_{31}, and p_{32} are path coefficients representing the causal impact of one variable upon another. The diagram can be represented by the following two equations; no equation is written for X_1 since it is considered an exogenous variable uninfluenced by any of the other measured variables:

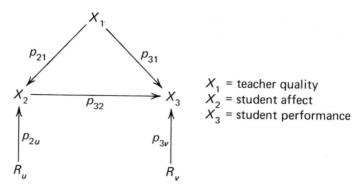

Figure 6-3. Recursive Model of Student Performance

$$X_2 = p_{21}X_1 + p_{2u}R_u \tag{6.1}$$

$$X_3 = p_{31}X_1 + p_{32}X_2 + p_{3v}R_v \tag{6.2}$$

Assumption 3 above says that R_u and X_1, R_v and X_1, and R_v and X_2 must be uncorrelated. Assumption 4 says there should not be any unmeasured variable (say X_4) that directly influences any two of our measured variables; otherwise, X_4 would have to be formally incorporated (measured) in the model to avoid possible misleading inferences.

Techniques for relaxing the first two assumptions are becoming more prominent so one should not despair of using causal techniques when there is interaction (i.e., nonadditive relationships) or when there is less than interval level data.[7] Also, nonlinear relationships can sometimes be made linear by an appropriate transformation.[8] The third and fourth assumptions are best justified by serious *substantive* reasoning by the investigator.

Once the path coefficients are estimated by ordinary regression techniques, the residual path coefficients representing the relationship between the unmeasured disturbance terms and their associated endogenous variables can be determined. This gives one a direct indicator of the explanatory power of the model. In addition to estimation, path analysis allows one to talk about the direct and indirect effects that one variable has upon another. For example, teacher quality (X_1) has a direct impact on student performance (X_3) and an indirect impact on performance via its impact on student affect (X_2). One can compute the magnitude of the direct and indirect effects that helps delineate the operative causal mechanisms.

In addition, with path analysis we can decompose the correlation between any two variables into a sum of simple and compound paths with some of the compound paths being substantively meaningful indirect effects and others perhaps not.[9] In our simple example, the only decomposition that can be performed that involves a substantively meaningful indirect effect is that between X_1 and X_3:

$$r_{13} = p_{31} + p_{21}p_{32}$$

Rank-ordering the components of the decomposition would again give us insight into the causal processes.

Finally, the decomposition of a correlation, in addition to yielding information about the causal processes, provides a way in which to test the adequacy of the model if some linkages have initially been omitted. If the model were specified correctly, then (except for measurement error and sampling error when relevant) the empirical correlation between any two variables should be numerically equal to the sum of the simple and compound paths linking the two variables. If the equality does not hold, this suggests that the model may be improperly specified and in need of revision. The most common type of revision is to include a linkage that was previously omitted. The major shortcoming of this procedure is that unguided by theoretical insight, one will likely end up with a model that includes all possible (recursive) linkages. If so, no model testing is possible as the model is exactly determined. The major shortcoming of a recursive model is its unrealistic omission of feedback processes, and thus we now turn our attention to nonrecursive path estimation.

Nonrecursive Path Estimation

Having shown that path analysis yields more information than arrow testing, we now turn to the often artificial and arbitrary distinctions drawn between recursive and nonrecursive estimation. While it is commonly agreed that models with nonrecursive (reciprocal) linkages more accurately reflect the complex processes of interest to us, it is also argued that nonrecursive models are generally more difficult to solve because of insufficient information. For example, our simple, three variable model of student performance might be more realistically depicted by the diagram and set of structural equations, shown in Figure 6-4, that formally incorporate the notion that stu-

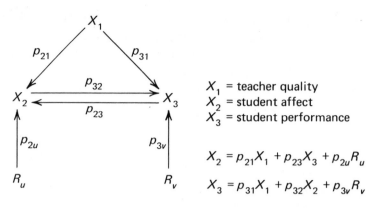

Figure 6-4. Nonrecursive Model of Student Performance

dent affect and student performance may mutually influence one another: Students with more positive affect are likely to perform better; conversely, students who perform better are likely to develop more positive affect.

As this model now stands, there is no way to get satisfactory estimates of the path coefficients. The main problem is that the error assumptions that were at least plausible in the recursive case are now totally implausible in the nonrecursive situation. For example, we would no longer expect R_u and X_3 to be uncorrelated since R_u has an indirect effect on X_3 via its impact on X_2. This means that our classical regression estimation techniques (and any other techniques) are no longer appropriate. In general, we say the model is underidentified, that there is insufficient information (or too many unknowns) to yield us a unique set of solutions. Hence, investigators often talk about the problem of identification in nonrecursive systems as if the problem was unique to such models. In fact, however, the problem is common to both recursive and nonrecursive systems; we unfortunately tend to assume it away in the former situation. Let us elaborate.

There are two basic ways of indentifying a system of equations: one by imposing limitations on the coefficients linking measured variables; the other by making certain assumptions about the correlations among the residual terms. These are generally called coefficient and covariance restrictions. In a recursive model, we always make many coefficient restrictions since we have set at least half of our coefficients equal to zero. For example, if in a recursive model we have said that X_1 influences X_2 (represented by p_{21}), we have implicitly set p_{12} equal to zero. Furthermore, in the recursive case, we are willing to make assumptions about error terms that, while unrealistic are not contradicted by the structure of the model. Whenever we make our usual assumptions about residual terms in a recursive model, we are guaranteed that our system of equations will be at least identified. In the nonrecursive case, we impose fewer restrictions upon the coefficients and covariances, thereby leading to more unknowns and greater difficulty in obtaining unique solutions.

It cannot be denied that nonrecursive equation systems present greater difficulties in estimation. But rather than viewing reciprocal models as difficult problems, we should treat them as opportunities to portray more adequately complex political processes and to avoid implausible assumptions. For example, in nonrecursive models we can allow the residual terms to be mutually correlated. Yet, the reader may ask, what good are reciprocal models if they cannot be estimated? Thus, our attention turns to strategies of making nonrecursive models tractable.

As mentioned above, there is no estimation technique appropriate for the nonrecursive version of our student performance model. In order to estimate the coefficients, we must find two exogenous variables, say X_a and X_b, that operate as indicated in Figure 6-5. According to the diagram, we must identify a variable X_a that only directly influences X_2 and a variable X_b that only affects X_3 directly. How do we find such variables? While desirable statistical properties of such exogenous variables have been discussed,[10] basically the search for such variables proceeds along substantive and theoretical grounds. We try to identify such variables according to our substantive and theoretical insights. But it is not sufficient simply to identify X_a and X_b; they must also be measured. This implies that at the design stage of our research we would have anticipated the need for X_a and X_b and therefore made plans to collect observations on each.

If a nonrecursive system is identified, then there are a variety of estimation techniques that one can use without an extensive econometrics background. There are, of course, important issues about optimal estimation techniques, particularly in the overidentified case where there is an excess of information. But this should not prevent the policy analyst from performing nonrecursive

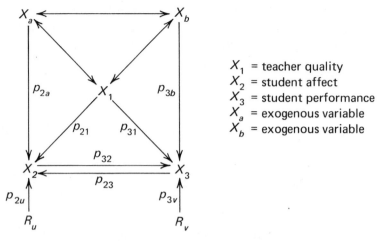

Figure 6-5. Five-Variable Nonrecursive Model of Student Performance

analysis using such widely accepted techniques as two stage least squares—available in many packages of computer programs.

Conclusion

Causal thinking, as reflected in the construction of arrow diagrams, is a significant task. However, if we cannot handle certain problems and meet certain assumptions, then analysis will be stymied, estimation impossible, and important questions unanswered. Indeed, we will often find ourselves in such a situation that causal modeling techniques cannot automatically be applied without some prior work on the part of the investigator. Among the problems that he must first surmount are the proper specification of models, often in areas where there is little solid theory upon which to build, and the satisfactory operationalization of key concepts. It was not our purpose here to go into strategies of model construction and operationalization except to say that the results of one's causal analysis are only as valid as the initial decisions made in building the model and operationalizing the variables.

We have argued in this chapter for the use of causal thinking and causal techniques in policy analysis. Even where the actual estimation cannot be performed, a causal style of thinking is still beneficial for theory building and hypothesis generation. Recursive and non-recursive path analysis procedures are important for they enable one to move beyond mindless correlation analysis and the simple estimation of direct effects, the basic output of ordinary regression. Rather, path analysis allows the investigator to examine the causal processes underlying his observed relationships and to get a handle on the relative importance of alternative paths of influence. The model testing permitted by path analysis procedures also encourages a more explicitly causal approach in the search for explanations of the phenomena under consideration. For all of these reasons, it appears that causal analysis holds substantial promise for policy studies.

Notes

1. See, for example, John Grumm, "The Effects of Legislative Structure on Legislative Performance," in Richard Hofferbert and Ira Sharkansky, eds., *State and Urban Politics* (Boston: Little, Brown and Company, 1971), pp. 298-322; Ira Sharkansky and Richard Hofferbert, "Dimensions of State Politics, Economics, and Public Policy," *The American Political Science Review* 63 (September 1969), pp. 867-79; and Donald S. Van Meter, "The Policy Implications of State Legislative Reapportionment: A Longitudinal Analysis," Ph.D. Diss. (Madison: University of Wisconsin, 1972).

2. See Grumm, "The Effects of Legislative Structure on Legislative Performance."

3. For an extended discussion of this issue, see Herbert B. Asher, "Some Problems in the Use of Multiple Indicators," paper prepared for the Conference on Design and Measurement Standards for Research in Political Science, Lake Lawn Lodge, Delevan, Wisconsin, May 13-15, 1974.

4. Elinor Ostrom, "The Need for Multiple Indicators in Measuring the Output of Public Agencies," *Policy Studies Journal* 2 (Winter 1973), pp. 87-92.

5. See, for example, Herbert Simon, "Spurious Correlation: A Causal Interpretation," in Herbert Simon, ed., *Models of Man* (New York: John Wiley & Sons, 1957), pp. 37-49; Hubert Blalock, *Causal Inferences in Nonexperimental Research* (Chapel Hill: Uni-

versity of North Carolina Press, 1964); Kenneth C. Land, "Princi-
ples of Path Analysis," in Edgar Borgatta, ed., *Sociological
Methodology 1969* (San Francisco: Jossey-Bass, 1969), pp. 3-37;
Otis Dudley Duncan, "Path Analysis: Sociological Examples,"
American Journal of Sociology 72 (July 1966), pp. 1-16; O. D.
Duncan, A. O. Haller, and A. Portes, "Peer Influences on Aspira-
tions: A Reinterpretation," *American Journal of Sociology* 74
(1968), pp. 119-37; Donald E. Stokes, "Compound Paths in Political
Analysis," in J. F. Herndon and J. L. Bernd, eds., *Mathematical
Applications in Political Science* 5 (Charlottesville: The University
Press of Virginia, 1971), pp. 70-92; and H. R. Alker, Jr., "Statistics
and Politics: The Need for Causal Data Analysis," in S. M. Lipset,
ed., *Politics and the Social Sciences* (New York: Oxford University
Press, 1969), pp. 244-313.

6. N. Draper and H. Smith, *Applied Regression Analysis* (New
York: John Wiley & Sons, 1966); and R. J. Wonnacott and T. H.
Wonnacott, *Econometrics* (New York: John Wiley Sons, 1970).

7. See T. P. Wilson, "Critique of Ordinal Variables," in H. M.
Blalock, ed., *Causal Models in the Social Sciences* (Chicago:
Aldine-Atherton, 1971); and R. P. Boyle, "Path Analysis and Ordinal Data," *American Journal of Sociology* 75 (September 1970), pp.
461-80.

8. See J. Strouse and J. O. Williams, "A Non-additive Model
for State Policy Research," *Journal of Politics* 34 (May 1972), pp.
648-57.

9. Donald E. Stokes, "Compound Paths in Political Analysis.

10. See, for example, Franklin M. Fisher, "The Choice of In-
strumental Variables in the Estimation of Economy-Wide
Econometric Models," in Hubert M. Blalock, Jr., ed., *Causal Models in the Social Sciences* (Chicago: Aldine-Atherton, 1971), pp.
245-72.

7

Assessing the Impact of Incremental Policies

E. Terrence Jones

During the past decade social scientists have become increasingly interested in using social science methodology to assess the extent to which public policies achieve their intended objectives. From a methodological viewpoint, this movement has been one of adapting research tools developed in other contexts to a new set of circumstances.

Up to now, most policy evaluation studies have dealt with major changes in policy. Such a concern is quite understandable since, if any policies are making a difference that can be detected by evaluation studies, it should be policies that have undergone a substantial transformation. The most frequent policies made by governments are not, however, major changes; instead, the most common governmental actions are regular (usually annual) shifts in expenditure and manpower levels. Many of these adjustments are intended to achieve changes in societal conditions; examples include police protection (minimize crime), fire protection (minimize fire damage), and health facilities and manpower (minimize mortality and morbidity). Thus, we can view such budgetary and personnel decisions as goal-oriented policies and proceed to evaluate their effectiveness. For instance, what impact do year-to-year changes in fire protection expenditures have on year-to-year changes in fire damage? This chapter discusses some of the research design, measurement, and data analysis problems involved in evaluating the impact of these everyday incremental policies.

Research Design

In the recent past, most policy impact studies have employed one of three designs: cross-sectional (e.g., the Coleman Report); a true experimental design involving randomized assignment of the independent variable (e.g., The New Jersey Graduated Work Incentive Experiment); and the quasi-experimental time series design (e.g.,

Campbell and Ross's evaluation of the Connecticut crackdown on speeding). None of these designs, however, is well-suited for assessing incremental policy impact. The cross-sectional design, by definition, does not include time as a variable and hence makes it more difficult to infer causation. The randomized experiment must be planned in advance, frequently presents ethical and political problems, and consequently can seldom be employed. Finally, the time series designs are by far best suited for major policy changes. Such designs need a minimum of three time series observations of the dependent variable both before and after the introduction of the new policy. Yet, budgetary and personnel changes occur so frequently that there are rarely more than one or two impact measure observations between one budgetary or personnel shift and the next. Using Campbell and Stanley's symbols—O's for the impact measurements (i.e., dependent variables) and X's for changes in policy (i.e., independent variable), with O subscripts representing time and X subscripts indicating different size changes in policy levels—the interrupted time-series representation is:

$$O_1 \; O_2 \; O_3 \; X \; O_4 \; O_5 \; O_6$$

whereas the budgetary and personnel change situation is:

$$O_1 \; X_3 \; O_2 \; X_1 \; O_3 \; X_2 \; O_4$$

The design that is most appropriate for evaluating the impact of everyday budgetary and personnel policies is a variant of the nonequivalent control group design. For a large number of similar groups (e.g., large cities, suburbs between 10,000 and 25,000 population, states), one takes a set of budgetary and/or personnel changes having a reasonable amount of variability and ascertains whether, for the entire set, there is any relationship between changes in the governmental actions and changes in the policy goal(s). Using the same symbols as above, this design's representation is:

$$O_1 \; X_2 \; O_2$$
$$O_1 \; X_1 \; O_2$$
$$O_1 \; X_0 \; O_2$$
$$O_1 \; X_{-1} \; O_2$$
$$O_1 \; X_{-2} \; O_2$$

It should be emphasized that the X's in the above design represent *changes* in expenditures or personnel levels from one period to the next and not a single static level of policy output. For example, O_1 might be Year T's infant mortality rate, O_2 Year $T + 1$'s infant mortality rate, and X the percentage increase in public health expenditures between Year $T-1$ and Year T.

Since this design is not a true experiment, randomization cannot be used to rule out all other possible causes. If competing causes of changes in the goals are to be ruled in or out, they must be measured and included in the analysis. In addition, since it is quite likely that budgetary and personnel changes will have more of an impact on their avowed goal(s) under some conditions than under others, it is highly important that appropriate conditional variables be included in the analysis. Two final problems with this design—clear specification of the variables' time-ordering and ruling out the common competing causes of population and income increases—are discussed in the data analysis section.

Measurement

The variables involved in an assessment of everyday policies are typically gathered from governmental sources. The United States Bureau of the Census's *Governmental Finances Series* has most of the expenditure data, and the same organization's *Government Employment Series* contains a wide range of personnel data. In addition, impact measures such as crime and health statistics are most commonly found in governmental records. Several questions should be asked (and satisfactorily answered) before using governmental data. First, is there an adequate fit between the governmental agency's operational definition and the concepts involved in the policy evaluation? Second, have there been changes in the governmental agency's operational definition over time and have such changes impaired or destroyed longitudinal comparability? Such changes, it must be added, are not always clearly noted; close scrutiny of definitions and sometimes correspondence with the agency itself are required to ferret them out. Third, aside from operational definitions, have there been other changes in the agency's data collection procedures (e.g., sampling) that might affect the measures?

A second measurement problem involved in assessing policy

impact is how to measure change in a variable from one period to the next. Absolute first differences $(X_2 - X_1)$ and relative first differences $[(X_2 - X_1)/X_1]$ are only two of the more obvious possibilities. Others, for instance, can be based on detrending methods or second and higher differences. A good discussion of these matters is Chester Harris's (ed.) *Problems in Measuring Change* (Madison: University of Wisconsin Press, 1963).

Data Analysis

In examining the relationship between changes in governmental expenditures or manpower and changes in various societal conditions, two common competing causes are changes in population and changes in economic well-being. Since randomization cannot generally be used to eliminate the influence of these latter two factors, some type of statistical control procedure must be employed. Although typically analysts would use either partial correlation or physical controls to accomplish the statistical task of controlling for the effects of a third variable on the relationship between the independent variable and the dependent variable, there is a common tendency when working with aggregate data to control by first dividing through the independent and dependent variables by the third variable (e.g., population) and then correlating the two indices (e.g., per capita health expenditures and per capita deaths). Unfortunately, such a procedure can sometimes generate erroneous results and it is better to use the more traditional control methods.

When analyzing data collected at a single point in time (i.e., cross-sectional data), there is seldom any choice as to how to relate two variables. When, however, time enters as a dimension (i.e., longitudinal data), the choices multiply. Is the hypothesized lag between changes in actions and subsequent changes in societal conditions one, two, three, or X periods? Or is the hypothesized causal impact distributed over several subsequent periods, in which instance several different lags must be tested? Is there an interaction effect among temporally adjacent government actions (e.g., in three successive time changes, do up-up-same or same-up-up patterns have more of an impact than a up-same-up record)? These are the kinds of questions that must be considered when investigating longitudinal relationships.

Conclusion

Since incremental adjustments are by far the most common type of policy changes made by governments, it is especially important that their possible effect(s) be assessed. To a large extent, the ability of present governments to change societal conditions depends on the ability of incremental adjustments in expenditures and manpower to achieve their declared objectives. Hence, in assessing incremental policies, we are in effect evaluating the modern polity's ability to improve the human condition.

8

Finding an Optimum Mix or Optimum Level for Public Policies

Stuart S. Nagel
University of Illinois

During the 1960's the most frequently used quantitative methodologies for analyzing public policies were cross-tabulation, correlation, and regression analysis in order to show the relation between policy causes and public policies or the relation between public policies and various goals or other effects. Merely knowing that certain policies bear a positive relation to desired goals, however, does not tell us what action to take (1) if our resources are such that we cannot adopt unlimited amounts of each policy, or (2) if adopting a good policy to an unlimited extent eventually reaches a point of diminishing absolute returns which we wish to avoid.

It is the purpose of this short article to describe some basic methodological concepts and techniques (1) for finding an optimum mix of public policies under scarce resources and (2) for finding an optimum level at which to operate a given public policy which has a hill-shaped relation with benefits or a U-shaped relation with costs. The concepts and techniques are largely taken from the literature of operations research and benefit-cost analysis.[1] Since that literature, however, mainly deals with examples from business, economics, and industrial engineering, one has to reason by analogy from it to political, legal, and sociological policy problems.

Finding an Optimum Policy Mix

a. With Linear Relations Between the Policies, Benefits, and Costs

Suppose we have the following basic cost-equation concerning a policy problem:

$$TC = P_1 + P_2 \tag{8.1}$$

This chapter originally appeared in *Policy Studies Journal* 2 (Winter 1973), no. 2, pp. 112-18.

where TC = total costs; P_1 = cost of the first policy activity or alternative; and P_2 = cost of the second policy activity or alternative. Suppose we also have the following basic benefits-equation:

$$TB = a + b_1 P_1 + b_2 P_2 \qquad (8.2)$$

where TB = total benefits; a = amount of benefits received if nothing is spent on P_1 or P_2; b_1 = the amount of change in the total benefits associated with an increase of one unit in P_1; and b_2 = the amount of change in the total benefits associated with an increase of one unit in P_2. The exact values of a, b_1, and b_2 can be determined by obtaining P_1, P_2, and TB scores for a number of different places or time-points and feeding that information into a computer regression analysis. Benefits can be measured in dollars, satisfaction expressed on an opinion survey, or by increases in equal opportunity or some other goal; just as costs can be measured in dollars, negative attitudes expressed on an opinion survey, or by increases in subjective effort or the expenditure of some other scarce resource unit.[a]

Suppose further that we want to find the optimum mix of expenditures for P_1 and P_2 so as to minimize TC or maximize TB subject to the following constraints or inequalities:

$$P_1 \; GEQ \; L_1 \qquad (8.3)$$

$$P_1 \; LEQ \; H_1 \qquad (8.4)$$

$$P_2 \; GEQ \; L_2 \qquad (8.5)$$

$$P_2 \; LEQ \; H_2 \qquad (8.6)$$

$$TC \; GEQ \; L_C \qquad (8.7)$$

$$TC \; LEQ \; H_C \qquad (8.8)$$

$$TB \; GEQ \; L_B \qquad (8.9)$$

$$TB \; LEQ \; H_B \qquad (8.10)$$

where GEQ = greater than or equal to; L = lowest limit which is desired, acceptable, or possible, for P_1, P_2, TC, or TB; LEQ = less than or equal to; and H = highest limit which is desired, acceptable, or possible for P_1, P_2, TC, or TB. In a real problem, numbers would

---

[a]One might want to add an additional basic equation to define net benefits or profits as $TPR = TB - TC$ where benefits and costs are measured in the same units. The formulas given in this article for maximizing total benefits could easily be adjusted, however, to apply to maximizing net benefits or profits.

be substituted for the symbols on the right side of inequalities (8.3) through (8.10).

Total cost may be minimized within the constraints by initially spending L_1 for P_1 and L_2 for P_2. With that allocation, however, we may not be spending enough to satisfy constraint number (8.9) which says TB should be greater than or equal to L_B. If so, then we should spend L_1 for P_1 and more than L_2 for P_2 if b_2 is greater than b_1. In other words, we should spend more for the policy alternative which has a closer relation or a greater slope with TB. The exact amount we should spend for P_2 (where b_2 GEQ b_1) can be determined by solving for the value of P_2 in the following equation:

$$L_B = a + b_1L_1 + b_2P_2 \qquad (8.11)$$

up to the point where $L_1 + P_2 = H_C$ so that we will not exceed our maximum budget available even though we may not have reached L_B. If, however, we raise P_2 up to H_2 and we still have not reached L_B, then we will have to raise P_1 as well, provided doing so will not result in $P_1 + H_2$ exceeding H_C. The value of an increased P_1 can be found by solving for P_1 in the following equation:

$$L_B = a + b_1P_1 + b_2H_2 \qquad (8.12)$$

Equations (8.11) and (8.12) logically follow from equation (8.2) which shows the relation between TB, P_1, and P_2.

Total benefits may be maximized within the constraints by initially spending H_1 for P_1 and H_2 for P_2. With that allocation, however, we may be spending too much to satisfy constraint number (8.8) which says TC should be less than or equal to H_C. If so, then we should spend H_2 for P_2 (where b_2 is GEQ b_1) and less than H_1 for P_1. In other words, spend less for the policy alternative which has a smaller relation or a lesser slope with TB. The exact amount we should spend for P_1 under these circumstances can be determined by solving for the value of P_1 in the following equation:

$$H_C = P_1 + H_2 \qquad (8.13)$$

If, however, we lower P_1 down to L_1 and we still have not reached H_C then we may have to lower P_2 as well. The exact value of P_2 under such circumstances can be determined by solving for P_2 in the following equation:

$$H_C = L_1 + P_2 \qquad (8.14)$$

Even if we lower P_2 to L_2, however, total costs may still exceed H_C meaning that in such a situation all the constraints cannot be satisfied simultaneously. Equations (8.13) and (8.14) logically follow from equation (8.1) which shows the relation between TC, P_1, and P_2.

Additional cost-minimization or benefit maximization situations may occur (depending on the numbers substituted for the L's, H's, b's, and the a), but one can generally see how they might be resolved by using the same kind of reasoning as was used in the above situations. Some situations may also involve solving for P_1 or P_2 in a system of simultaneous equations and inequalities rather than a single equation like equations (8.11) through (8.14). For example, suppose one wanted to find the value of P_1 in equation (8.12) without violating the constraint that TC LEQ H_C (i.e., $P_1 + H_2$ LEQ H_C). With only two policies, the problem can be resolved by graphing the constraints (8.3) through (8.10) on a two dimensional graph with P_1 on one axis and P_2 on the other. In graphing the TC constraints (8.7) and (8.8), substitute $P_1 + P_2$ for TC. In graphing the TB constraints ((8.9) and (8.10)), substitute $a + b_1P_1 + b_2P_2$ for TB. With more than two policies the problem can be resolved by a linear programming computer routine available at most large computing centers.[b]

b. With Non-Linear Relations

Suppose instead of benefits-equation (8.2), the relations between TB, P_1, and P_2 are as follows:

$$TB = a \cdot (P_1)^{b_1} \cdot (P_2)^{b_2} \qquad (8.15)$$

where a = amount of benefits received if only one unit of expenditure is spent on P_1 and one unit on P_2; b_1 = a decimal number to which P_1 is raised to show the degree of diminishing marginal benefits from additional units of P_1; and b_2 = a decimal number to which P_2 is raised to show the degree of diminishing marginal benefits from additional units of P_2. The exact values of a, b_1, and b_2 can be determined by (1) obtaining P_1, P_2, and TB scores for a number of

[b]When we find an optimum mix between alternative policies, we are really making the ratio of marginal benefits to marginal costs equal for all our policies. In that context, the TC equation [(8.1)] can be thought of as one of a series of consumption possibility lines, and the TB equation [(8.2)] as one of a series of indifference lines. Geometrically, our obect is to find the furthest in or smallest TC line that will satisfy TB constraint [(8.9)], or to find the furthest out TB line that will satisty TC constraint [(8.8)].

different places or time-points, (2) determining the logarithms of P_1, P_2, and TB, and then (3) feeding that information into a computer regression analysis.

Suppose further the basic cost-equation (8.1) still holds true and that we want to find the optimum mix of expenditures for P_1 and P_2 so as to *minimize TC* subject to constraint nine which establishes a minimum benefit level. With these givens, the optimum amount to spend (i.e., equation (8.16) for $P_1 = b_1/b_2$ times L_B/a, where b_1/b_2 is raised to the power of $b_2/(b_1 + b_2)$, and where L_B/a is raised to the power of $1/(b_1 + b_2)$. Once one has determined P_1 from this equation (8.16), then one can determine P_2 by subtracting P_1 from TC in light of equation (8.1). This equation (8.16) was arrived at by using the rules of elementary calculus to find the slope of TC relative to P_1 given equation (8.1), but expressing P_2 in terms of P_1 by way of equation (8.15) with TB in equation (8.15) set at L_B. One then sets the formula for that slope equal to zero (the point at which the slope has bottomed out or stopped changing) and then solves for P_1 in terms of the other variables.

Suppose now that we want to find the optimum mix of expenditures for P_1 and P_2 so as to *maximize TB* subject to constraint (8.8) which establishes a maximum total cost line. With these givens, the optimum amount to spend (i.e., equation (8.17) for $P_1 = b_1$ times $1/b_2$ times P_2 with the P_2 raised to a power equal to $1 + 2b_2$, and with the product resulting from multiplying those three terms together raised to a power equal to $1/1(1 + 2b_1)$. When the numerical values of b_1 and b_2 are filled in via the above mentioned regression analysis, then equation (8.17) gives us the ratio of optimum P_1 to optimum P_2. Thus, if it shows $P_1 = 3P_2$, then $H_C = 3P_2 + P_2$, and $P_2 = H_C/4$. This equation (8.17) was arrived at by using the rules of elementary calculus to find the slope of TB relative to P_1 given equation (8.15) but expressing P_2 in terms of P_1 by way of equation (8.1) with TC in equation (8.1) set at H_C. One then sets the formula for that slope equal to zero (the point at which the slope has peaked or stopped changing) and then solves for P_1 in terms of the other variables.

If we re-insert all the constraints (8.3) through (8.10) which we have not been considering, the problem of finding the optimum allocation between P_1 and P_2 given equation (8.15) becomes substantially more complicated. The optimum allocation can, however, be arrived at with an eyeball estimation by graphing all the constraints with $P_1 + P_2$ substituted for TC and $a \cdot (P_1)^{b_1} \cdot (P_2)^{b_2}$ substituted for

TB. More exact determinations can be made by the use of what are known as Lagrange multipliers or by non-linear programming computer routines. Such routines may be essential to handling the problem of non-linear policy relations where there are more than two policies unless the policies can be dichotomized.

Finding an Optimum Level

Suppose we have the following rising-cost equation concerning a problem of how much of a policy to adopt:

$$TCP = a_1(P)^{b_1} \tag{8.18}$$

where P = percentage or amount of total available effort expended in pursuing a policy (e.g., percentage of defendants held prior to trial); TCP = total or average social cost of pursuing a policy (e.g., cost of *holding* defendants in jail prior to trial); a_1 = amount of TCP incurred if only one unit of effort is expended in pursuing the policy (e.g., if only one percent of the defendants are held prior to trial); and b_1 = a positive number to which P is raised to show the degree of increasing TCP costs from additional units of P.

Suppose we also have the following falling-cost equation with regard to the same policy problem:

$$TCQ = a_2(P)^{b_2} \tag{8.19}$$

where TCQ = total or average social cost of pursuing an opposite policy (e.g., cost of rearresting a *released* defendant who fails to appear for trial); a_2 = amount of TCQ incurred if only one unit of effort is expended in pursuing the policy; and b_2 = a negative number to which P is raised to show the degree of falling TCQ costs from additional units of P.

Suppose further we have the following total cost equation based on equations (8.18) and (8.19).

$$TC = TCP + TCQ \tag{8.20}$$

where TC = total costs of pursuing a policy which incurs high costs if too little or too much of the policy is pursued. Note the level problem as discussed here uses policies that have a U-shaped relation to total costs. By analogy, however, one could apply the reasoning used to policies that have a hill-shaped relation to total benefits or to total benefits minus costs.

The optimum level of P at which the U-shaped total cost curve reaches a bottom point is the point (i.e., equation (8.21) where $P = (a_2b_2)/(a_1b_1)$, with that ratio raised to the power $1/(b_1 + b_2)$. If $b_1 = b_2$, the ratio part of equation (8.21) simplifies to a_2/a_1, and optimum P is then at the point where $TCP = TCQ$.

The exact values of a_1, b_1, a_2, and b_2 can be determined by the same kind of data gathering and regression analysis which was mentioned in describing the non-linear mixing problem. Equation (8.21) is derived by using elementary calculus rules to find the slope of TC relative to P in equation (8.20) (with the expression from equation (8.18) substituted for TCP and the expression from equation (8.19) substituted for TCQ), and then setting that slope equal to zero and algebraically solving for P.[c]

Either equation (8.18) or (8.19) could be changed to show a linear rather than an exponential relation with TCP or TCQ. For example, if just equation (8.18) were changed so $TCP = a_1 + b_1P$, then the optimum P level (derived through the calculus approach) $= -b_1(a_2b_2)$, with that ratio raised to the power $1/(b_2 - 1)$. If $b_2 = -1$ (which means that TCP is a straight line and TCQ is a rectanglular hyperbola), then optimum P = the square root of a_2/b_1, and optimum P is at the point where $TCP = TCQ$. If both TCP and TCQ were straight-line relations, then optimum P would be 0 percent when the absolute value of b_1 is greater than the absolute value of b_2. In the opposite case, optimum P is 100 percent, or else optimum P is the percent at which TCQ reaches zero if that percent is less than 100 percent. There is no optimum P with all straight-line costs where $b_1 = b_2$ since any value of P will then produce the same TC.

The level problem can be made less simple by adding constraints which specify lower and upper limits for P other than zero percent and 100 percent. With such constraints, Lagrange multipliers or non-linear programming routines may be applicable like those mentioned in discussing the non-linear mixing problem. Graphing, however, may provide a sufficiently accurate and insight-provoking approach to such problems. The level problem can also be made more complicated by having equations (8.18) or (8.19) generate cost

---

[c]When we minimize total costs in the context of finding an optimum level, we are really minimizing total losses or maximizing total profits. This is so since profits = benefits − costs, and losses = negative benefits + costs when we multiply the profit equation through by minus one. In our example, negative benefits are referred to as releasing costs, and costs are referred to as holding costs. When one maximizes profits, marginal or incremental profits equal zero, and marginal benefits equal marginal costs. Thus when one minimizes losses, marginal losses equal zero, and negative marginal releasing costs equal marginal holding costs.

curves with multiple bends, but such curves are too unrealistic in the real world to be worthy of extensive analysis. The U-shaped total cost curve is, however, a common policy phenomena, as illustrated by (1) the pretrial release problem; (2) the problem of finding an optimum integration level (where one avoids both the opportunity costs of tokenism and the re-segregation costs of pushing integration too far); (3) the enforcement of anti-pornography laws (where some feel too little enforcement may result in undesirable sexual distraction or provocation and too much enforcement may spill over into political and literary censorship); and (4) other policy problems.

Likewise, the mixing problem frequently occurs in the real world. For example, (1) what is the optimum mix between law reform and case handling in running the OEO legal services program; (2) what is the optimum way to allocate funds to different geographical areas in order to maximize total national benefits; (3) what is the optimum way to allocate precincts to districts in order to provide equal population per legislative district; and (4) what is the optimun mix of civil rights efforts in the fields of voting, employment, education, housing, public accomodations, and criminal justice. It is hoped that policy studies researchers will continue to show increasing concern for compiling data and developing models designed to get at the optimum mix and optimum levels for diverse public policies, and also designed to compare and account for the differences between the optimum and the empirical in public policy-making.

Notes

1. For further detail on the methodologies discussed in this article, see Samuel Richmond *Operations Research for Management Decisions* (Ronald Press, 1968); William Baumol, *Economic Theory and Operations Analysis* (Prentice-Hall, 1965); and E. J. Mishan, *Cost-Benefit Analysis* (Praeger, 1971). For examples of public policy research using an optimum mix methodology, see Charles Laidlaw, *Linear Programming for Urban Development Plan Evaluation* (Praeger, 1972); and Stuart Nagel, *Minimizing Costs and Maximizing Benefits in Providing Legal Services to the Poor* (Sage Professional Papers in Adminstrative and Policy Studies, 1973). Examples using an optimum levels methodology

include, G. Becker, "Crime and Punishment: An Economic Approach," 76 *Journal of Political Economy* 169 (1968); and S. Nagel & P. Wice, "The Policy Problem of Doing Too Much or Too Little: Pre-Trial Release as a Case in Point" (Sage Professional Papers in Administrative and Policy Studies, 1975).

9 Experimental Design in Policy Impact Analysis

*Frank P. Scioli, Jr. and
Thomas J. Cook*

An increasingly prominent aspect of policy analysis has been the scholarly attention directed towards research which focuses upon the measurement of the effects of public policy decisions: policy impact analysis.[1] Within this body of literature a recurring debate has centered upon the applicability of alternative research methodologies to the analysis of policy impacts—in particular, the application of experimental design principles within the naturalistic (i.e., non-laboratory) research milieu endemic to social policy research. Our objective in this paper is not to join the debate, but rather to delineate the main points of contention and propose a generalized research design that accommodates both perspectives. The flexibility of the proposed design will be discussed in terms of its utility under varying conditions of data availability.

The Utility of Experimental Design

The call for the application of experimental design principles to social policy evaluation reflects the interdisciplinary appeal of this research technique. Economists, sociologists, psychologists and even political scientists have argued that experimental design methodology offers the greatest opportunity for determining what, if any, causal linkages exist between policy action and policy impact.[2] This opportunity rests on the main characteristic of experimental research: prior control by the researcher over the components of his research design.[3] This control is manifested in several ways particularly relevant to impact analysis. For example, the determination of who participates in a particular program, the type of participation, and the level of participation are all conditions potentially within the researcher's control.

Reprinted, with permission, from *Social Science Quarterly*, vol. 54 (September 1973).

    This article is part of an ongoing collaborative stream of research in which we are alternating the order of authors' names to indicate that the studies are in every way joint efforts.

An example of this type of control can be seen in some of the design considerations involved in a recent household allowance experiment.[4] This experiment involves the following design components: program variations (v), characteristics of household influencing housing choices (c), characteristics of market and public policies influencing housing choices (m), and, household response measures (i.e., housing choices) (y). The objective of the experiment is to determine the value for the response measures within the functional expression $y = f(v,c,m)$. One method utilized in the experiment for determining this value of y is a 3^2 factorial design. The advantage of this experimental design is the fact that the researchers have control over the assignment of individuals to various program variations. Further, since assignment to program variations is on the basis of a randomization procedure the investigators have eliminated the possibility that factors beyond their control, or unknown to them, will confound their results. As Campbell points out:

The magic of randomization is that it attenuates the causal threads of the past as they might codetermine both exposure to the treatment and gain scores. Randomization renders implausible innumerable rival explanations of the observed change by cutting the lawful relationships which in the natural setting would determine which person gets which treatment. This provides the persuasive "causal" interpretations made possible by experiments involving randomization.[5]

Concomitant with this feature of control is the ability to assess the interactive, as well as independent, effects of policy action. This is crucial for impact analysis. Albeit, the analysis is concerned with the total impact of a program across all individuals and all program sites, the more important question concerns the uniformity of impacts across varying program conditions (i.e., individuals, program variations, program sites). A recent study by Light found that the impact of participation in a Head Start program was not constant across all program sites.[6] Variables such as center personnel and the characteristics of the children in a center were found to be related to the performance of children on the selected criterion measures. Light notes that the conclusions reached in the Westinghouse Report failed to specify the conditions under which the Head Start experience *did* produce changes in the criterion measures. Thus, a focus on the total impact of the program across all program sites failed to reveal an important interactive component involved in the operation of Head Start centers. Had the Westinghouse evaluators cast their analysis within a factorial design rationale, for example, they would have been able to measure the total impact of the program. More importantly, they would also have been able to determine the specific conditions (e.g., center personnel and participant characteristics) under which program participation did produce significant changes in children's performance.[a]

Limitations to the Application of Experimental Design Methodology

Despite the advantages pointed out above, the acceptance of experimental design methodology is not universal within the area of policy evaluation. The primary criticism centers on the following points: (1) the impracticality of introducing experimental procedures within an applied (i.e., action) research setting; (2) the inability of experimental design procedures to evaluate the total policy process; and (3) the limited generalizability of experimental results to non-experimental settings (i.e., external validity).

The first criticism is based upon the reluctance of many administrators to accept (or adhere to) the design requirements imposed by an experimental analysis of program effects. The requirement of randomly assigning individuals to program variations is particularly disturbing to administrators.[7] The criticism ranges from the charge that random assignment is a poor substitute for "professional judgment" to the assertion that such a procedure substitutes statistical theory for personal, individualized selection (i.e., is "inhumane"). This criticism has been translated, in at least one instance, into a prohibition against randomization as a means of program assignment. Peter Rossi cites a provision of the Elementary and Secondary Education Assistance Act of 1965 which specifically enjoined random assignment as a means of determining participation in one of the authorized program variations.[8]

The second criticism cites the limitation of experimental design methodology as *the* approach to program evaluation. The critics contend that experimental methodology, in its exclusive focus upon

---

[a]In terms of the experimental design, center personnel and participant characteristics were nested factors within the overall design. For an elaboration of this point see Houston, "The Behavioral Sciences Impact."

performance criteria as the measure of program effects, overlooks many key aspects of program operation vital to an overall assessment of program performance. Daniel Stufflebeam, in discussing educational evaluation, limits the utility of experimental design to input and product evaluation situations.[9] Questions such as the feasibility of program objectives, time factors in program operation, staff competence and efficient resource utilization, etc., while important to assessing program performance, are not tractable through an experimental design approach. This critique, of course, reflects Stufflebeam's perception of the scope of evaluation research.[b]

The final criticism is not peculiar to evaluation research, but rather has been leveled at the general applicability of experimentation within the social sciences, i.e., the generalization of experimental findings to other social settings. Two points are generally made to substantiate this claim.[10] First, the extent of program control and specificity required by experimental design are not realized within the social setting in which a program generally operates. In other words, the "real world" is not structured like an experiment but rather, exists as an amorphous configuration of people, places, and things. Second, the operation of most social action programs is best conceptualized through an evolutionary framework. Thus, the operation of a program at any one point in time is a function of a developmental process resulting from program modification to meet situational exigencies. The necessity of design stability in experimental research precludes application within the protean environment of social action research, an environment of changing personnel, participants, and program constraints.

A Proposed Design Alternative

The objective of this paper is to seek an optimum methodological mid-point between the two positions outlined above: to wit, a proposed design alternative which maximizes the advantages cited in connection with the experimental approach while, at the same time, recognizing the limitations inherent in social action research. The design is presented in terms of its general utility and appropriateness

---

[b]The argument has been offered that evaluation research is concerned with a narrower focus upon the performance criteria. See, for example, Carol H. Weiss, *Evaluation Research* Englewood Cliffs, New Jersey: Prentice-Hall, 1972), pp. 66-67.

Table 9-1
Trend Analysis Design[a]

Drugs	Subjects	Trials		
		B_1	B_2	B_3
A_1	1	$A_1S_1B_1$		
	2			
	3			
	4			
	5			
A_2	1		$A_2S_1B_2$	
	2			
	3			
	4			
	5			
A_3	1			$A_3S_1B_3$
	2			
	3			
	4			
	5			

Where A = Treatment Condition
    B = Trial or Time Period
    S = Subject or Experimental Unit

[a]Allen L. Edwards, *Experimental Design in Psychological Research* (New York: Holt, Rinehart and Winston, 1960), p. 229. [Table 9-1] is a slightly modified display of Edwards' design.

for policy impact analysis. Specific application is, of course, contingent upon the data characteristics of the particular program being evaluated, a point discussed more fully below.

The basis for the design relies in part, upon a trend analytic approach.[11] In its adaptation to program evaluation the design focuses on *the impact of program alternatives across specific time periods in different locations.* The adaptation is based upon the following rationale underlying systematic program evaluation: (1) the measurement of program impacts across specific time periods; (2) the comparison of alternative programs across specific time periods; (3) the measurement of the *main* and *interactive* impacts of programs through the introduction of control parameters; and (4) the determination of the linearity of program impacts.

In its original form as displayed in Table 9-1, the trend analysis design permits a determination of (1) the main versus the interactive effects of treatment conditions, and (2) the linear component of the trend. The first determination is important as a measure of both the independent effects of single treatments and the relative effects of

Table 9-2A

Program	Units	Time Intervals I_{-6} I_{-5} I_{-4} I_{-3} I_{-2} I_{-1} I_1 I_2 I_3 I_4 I_5 I_6
P_1	T_1	
	T_2	
	T_3	
	C_1	
P_2	T_1	
	T_2	
	T_3	
	C_1	
P_3	T_1	
	T_2	
	T_3	
	C_1	
⋮		
P_n		

Baseline   Treatment

alternative treatments. The design specifically allows for tests of interaction between treatments, trials (i.e., time periods), and included control variables. The linear component determination is a measure of the constancy of treatment effects across a specifiable time dimension. Edwards suggests how this may be examined both statistically (through the sum of squares due to a linear trend) and visually (through the plotting of criterion measures against trials). A significant non-linear (e.g., quadratic) trend in the treatment effects indicates interaction between treatments and trials (or time intervals) and allows refinement in the interpretation of treatment effects. A significant quadratic component, for example, negates the assertion of constancy of treatment effects across time.

The design presented in Tables 9-2A, 2B, 2C is a modification of the basic trend analysis design in three main aspects. The first modification was the inclusion of an extended pre-treatment dimen-

Table 9-2B

Unit	Control Variable	I_{-n}	$\cdots$	I_{-3}	I_{-2}	I_{-1}	I_1	I_2	I_3	$\cdots$	I_n
					Time					**Intervals**	
$C_1 \ldots C_n$	CV_1										
	CV_2										
	CV_3										
	CV_4										
	$\vdots$										
	CV_n										
$T_1 \ldots T_n$	CV_1										
	CV_2										
	CV_3										
	CV_4										
	$\vdots$										
	CV_n										

P_1

Baseline   Treatment

sion (i. e., baseline) as a means of measuring the stability of the criterion measures prior to the intervention of the treatment conditions. As in the Connecticut Crackdown Study,[12] most social programs represent interventions into the social system in attempting to alleviate specific problems. Since the problem invariably will have existed at different levels of intensity prior to the intervention period, any attempt to assess the impact of the intervention would have to take into consideration the pre-treatment variability of the criterion measures. The second modification involves the inclusion of control group units (C_1) to extend the baseline period into the treatment time frame. This provides a constant comparative assessment of the stability of the criterion measures in the absence of the treatment condition(s).

The third modification, interval expansion, refers to the program structure characteristic of most social action policy. Seldom does the researcher encounter a program consisting of a single, objective

Table 9-2C

	Control	Level	Time								Intervals	
			I_n	$\ldots$	I_{-3}	I_{-2}	I_{-1}	I_1	I_2	I_3	$\ldots$	I_n
T_1	CV_1	L_1										
		L_2										
		L_3										
	CV_2	L_1										
		L_2										
		L_3										
	CV_n	L_1										
		$\vdots$										
		L_n										

Baseline   Treatment

Definition of Symbols—

Program: $(P_1 \ldots P_n)$ = specific program alternatives directed towards stated objectives.

Treatment Units: $(T_1 \ldots T_n)$ = specific targets of program activity. Could refer, for example, to persons residing in selected cities.

Control Units: $(C_1 \ldots C_n)$ = persons (or groups) randomly assigned to control status within a given target area (e.g., city).

Time Intervals—Baseline $(I_{-6} \ldots I_{-1})$ = observations on criterion measures prior to the intervention of program activity.

—Treatment $(I_1 \ldots I_n)$ = observations on criterion measures after intervention of program activity.

Control Variables: $(CV_1 \ldots CV_n)$ = control parameters included into the design which bear a hypothesized relationship to the program activity—program impact relationship.

Control Variable Levels: $(L_1 \ldots L_n)$ = levels of control variables that may contain an interactive component.

program activity, and one measure of program effectiveness. Rather, most programs entail a multiplicity of objectives, activities, and criterion measures.[13] The possibility of multiple activities with multiple criterion measures may necessitate sub-classification and analysis within each time interval to assess the extent of suboptimization nested in the overall program impact matrix. That is, the relative contributions of each program activity to the overall program impact.

The reader will note that the progression from Table 9-2A to Table 9-2C is in terms of analytical refinement. Table 9-2B introduces specific control variables hypothesized as important to the measurement of program impact. Table 9-2C refines the control variables in terms of levels of control. The researchers' point of entry into the Table 9-2A to Table 9-2C sequence depends, of course, on the characteristics of the data base upon which the analysis is grounded. It may be, for example, that data limitations restrict analysis to the Table 9-2A level of investigation. Thus, the more extensive the data base the greater the analytical specificity permitted by the design. The value of this type of refinement is underscored by Light's criticism discussed above: the specification of program effects as a function of program implementation conditions. Thus, the question is not just "does the program have an effect?" but, moreover, "what is the effect of the program under varying, and relevant, conditions of program implementation?"

The design presented in Tables 9-2A-2C is specifically directed at the following set of questions:

(1) What are the main impacts of *single* programs over time $(I_1 \ldots I_n)$ relative to the behavior of criterion measures in control units?

(2) What are the relative impacts of programs $(P_1 \ldots P_n)$ over time upon the common policy objectives?

(3) Can the relationship between program activity and criterion measure behavior be expressed as a linear function?

(4) Is there significant interaction between program activity, program environment $(CV_1 \ldots CV_n)$, program units (e.g., cities) and time interval(s)?

As was stated above, the application of the proposed design is contingent upon the data available, or potentially available, within the research setting of the program to be evaluated. One may conceptualize a continuum of application possibilities ranging from the true experiment to the use of archival data. Utilization of the design as a true experiment requires that the researcher satisfy the following conditions. (1) The random assignment of individuals to treatment and control groups; (2) Independence of treatments. The latter requirement is important to avoid contamination between, for example, different treatments (i.e., program variations) and also between program participants and selected control groups.[14] The pretreatment period $(I_{-6} \ldots I_{-1})$ is included to insure a stable baseline from which inferences concerning behavior change may be made.

The analytical refinement component in the design cautions the researcher to plan ahead for the necessary sample size to adequately utilize the cells in the matrix. The latter point is particularly relevant to applications where a true experiment is precluded. In these situations, where the data base is that of a time-series, the pre-treatment period provides a means of assessing the stability of the criterion measures prior to program intervention.[c] While in the true experiment, random assignment obviates some of the necessity for explicit inclusion of control variables, the more remote a particular research project is from this ideal the greater the need for specification, and inclusion, of control variables in the research design. The proposed design stresses the careful consideration of relevant control variables at the outset. Thus, whether one's research problem meets the requisites of a true experiment or the analyst must rely upon archival data generated by others, control over the components of the research problem is a desired goal. The proposed design affords an opportunity for realizing this goal in both the true experiment setting and under conditions of *ex post facto* analysis.

Conclusion

In this paper we have addressed the central question of policy impact analysis: Did the policy decision, as implemented through specific program activities, have a measurable impact upon the target population consistent with the policy objectives? The pros and cons of experimental design methodology vis-à-vis this question were discussed and a design alternative to a true experiment was proposed.

The latter design was presented in terms of its general utility for impact analysis. For the academic researcher, it affords a means of organizing his data to measure impacts both across and within delimitable time periods. For the practitioners, it could serve an additional function. The design affords a framework for the continuous monitoring of program effectiveness. By a continuous updating of the cells in the matrix as new observations on performance criteria become available, the program administrator has a running record of program performance. Thus, by using the impact matrix as a "data-generating" mechanism the administrator will have a co-

[c]Campbell's point on the regression artifact problem is relevant here. See his "Reforms as Experiments."

herent evidential base upon which to make decisions concerning continuance, modification, or cessation of a given program activity. Moreover, the matrix facilitates data management for more sophisticated mathematical-statistical analysis. As was pointed out above, the design is flexible in its potential application to different research problems; it is constrained primarily by the data available within different program operation settings.

Notes

1. For an excellent annotated bibliography on this topic see Carol H. Weiss, et al., "Abstracts on Evaluation Research." Model Cities Evaluation Institute, U.S. Department of Housing and Urban Development, May, 1971. See also Peter H. Rossi and Walter Williams, eds., *Evaluating Social Programs* (New York: Seminar Press, 1972).

2. For examples of the interdisciplinary appeal of the experimental approach see: G. H. Orcutt and A. G. Orcutt, "Incentive and Disincentive Experimentation for Income Maintenance Policy Purposes," *American Economic Review,* 58 (Sept., 1968), pp. 754-772; Donald T. Campbell, "Reforms as Experiments," *American Psychologist,* 24 April, 1969), pp. 409-429; Glen G. Cain and Robinson G. Hollister, *Evaluating Manpower Programs for the Disadvantaged* (Madison: Institute for Research on Poverty, University of Wisconsin, 1969); Tom R. Houston, Jr., "The Behavioral Sciences Impact—Effectiveness Model," paper presented at the Seminar on Evaluation Research, American Academy of Arts and Sciences, 1969; Thomas J. Cook and Frank P. Scioli, Jr., "A Research Strategy for Analyzing the Impact of Public Policy," *Administrative Science Quarterly,* 17 (Sept., 1972), pp. 328-339.

3. D. J. Finney, *Theory of Experimental Design* (Chicago: University of Chicago Press, 1960); William G. Cochran and Gertrude G. Cox, *Experimental Designs* (New York: John Wiley & Sons, 1957).

4. Garth Buchanan and John Heinberg, "Housing Allowance Household Experiment Design: Part 1, Summary and Overview," working paper, The Urban Institute, Washington, D.C., May 22, 1972.

5. Donald T. Campbell, "From Description to Experimenta-

tion," in Chester W. Harris, ed., *Problems in Measuring Change* (Madison: University of Wisconsin Press, 1963), p. 213.

6. Richard J. Light and Paul V. Smith, "Choosing a Future: Strategies for Designing and Evaluating New Programs," *Harvard Education Review,* 40 (Winter, 1970), pp. 1-28.

7. Peter H. Rossi, "Testing for Success and Failure in Social Action," in Rossi and Williams, eds., *Evaluating Social Programs,* pp. 30-31.

8. Ibid., p. 31.

9. Daniel L. Stufflebeam, "The Use of Experimental Design in Educational Evaluation," paper read at the National Convention of the American Educational Research Association, Minneapolis, Minnesota, March, 1970.

10. For an elaboration of these points see Robert S. Weiss and Martin Rein, "The Evaluation of Broad-Aim Programs: A Cautionary Case and a Moral," *Annals of the American Academy of Political and Social Sciences,* 385 (1969), pp. 133-142; and Robert S. Weiss and Martin Rein, "The Evaluation of Broad-Aim Programs: Experimental Design, Its Difficulties, and an Alternative," *Administrative Science Quarterly,* 15 (June, 1970), pp. 97-109. For a reply to this argument see, Donald T. Campbell, "Considering the Case against Experimental Evaluations of Social Innovations," *Administrative Science Quarterly,* 15 (June, 1970), pp. 110-113.

11. See Allen L. Edwards, *Experimental Design and Psychological Research* (New York: Holt, Rinehart and Winston, 1960), pp. 224-253.

12. Donald T. Campbell and H. Laurence Ross, "The Connecticut Crackdown on Speeding: Time Series Data in Quasi-Experimental Analysis," *Law and Society Review,* (Aug., 1968), pp. 33-53.

13. For a discussion of this conceptualization see Robert J. Mowitz, *The Design and Implementation of Pennsylvania's Planning, Programming, Budgeting System* (University Park, Pa.: The Institute of Public Administration, The Pennsylvania State University, 1970), pp. 14-22, and Cook and Scioli, "A Research Strategy," pp. 330-331.

14. For an excellent discussion of this problem see George A. Fairweather, *Methods For Experimental Social Innovation* (New York: John Wiley, 1967).

**Part IV
Analysis**

Introduction to Part IV

Part IV discusses some of the issues surrounding the analysis of data generated during the course of a policy study. Chapter 10 by L. A. Wilson II and chapter 11 by Thomas R. Dye and Neuman F. Pollack follow closely the chapters on time series design and causal modeling included in Part III. The statistical procedures associated with these approaches are discussed in detail, and, in the Dye and Pollack chapter, the discussion is illustrated with a substantive example from the criminal justice field: identifying the determinants of police protection in American cities. Chapter 12 by James W. Dyson and Douglas St. Angelo raises a methodological issue concerning the suitability of the correlational procedures as applied to research in the policy output area, in particular, the situation where the researcher wants to assess the relationship between a dependent variable, such as state spending policies, and a hypothesized causal antecendent variable, such as socioeconomic environmental factors. Their conclusions challenge the assertion that the taxing and spending policies of a state may be a function of the state's socioeconomic environment, a conclusion that is widely held in much of the policy output literature. Chapter 13 by Ronald W. Johnson and John M. Pierce cuts across much of the foregoing discussion in the book in detailing the issues relevant to measurement, design, and analysis in applying an economic perspective, cost-benefit/effectiveness analysis, to the study of public policy. The Johnson and Pierce chapter underscores the need to approach the study of public policy, in this case policy impact analysis, from an interdisciplinary perspective with the goal of optimizing the fit between methodology and substantive focus.

10 Statistical Techniques for the Analysis of Public Policies as Time Series Quasi-experiments

L. A. Wilson II

A seldom used but frequently appropriate approach to the evaluation of the impact of public policy is that of formulating the research in the context of a quasi-experimental, interrupted time series design. Thomas J. Cook and Frank P. Scioli, Jr. in noting the lack of "rigorous assessments of the impact of public policy," (1972, pp. 7-8) within the field of political science, have made a similar observation: "With rare exception the investigations (to date) have been ex post facto analyses with little attention given to the advantages of experimental and quasi-experimental designs for conducting the analysis." Of the many reasons that might explain this neglect, at least a few should be mentioned here. It may be, as James A. Caporaso and Alan L. Pelowski suggest, that political scientists "feel that the neat procedures applicable to the isolated laboratory are not appropriate for the messy, *ex post facto* research problems which confront us" (1971, p. 418). Or, perhaps as Caporaso and Pelowski also note, this neglect may arise from "confusing the *logic* of experimentation with its procedures and techniques" (1971, p. 418).

While it is true that most public policy research is "messy" as compared with the closely controlled laboratory situation, many quasi-experimental designs have been articulated by social scientists that are appropriate for many types of social science research endeavors and the merits of these designs have been recognized for some time. It is not denied, however, that some of the procedures and techniques of these designs are confusing. This chapter is intended to acquaint the reader with both the procedures of quasi-experimental time series design and some of the statistical techniques currently available for the evaluation of public policy in this context. The purpose of this chapter is not, as some might suggest, to make the method "the independent variable, the problem the dependent one" (Fairweather 1967, p. 16) but rather to expedite the integration of problem and method to the advantage of the social science researcher.

As Donald T. Campbell points out, "The essence of the time series design is the presence of a periodic measurement process on some group or individual and the introduction of an experimental change into this time series of measurements, the results of which are indicated by a discontinuity in the measurements recorded in the time series: (1967, p. 220). A second similar design, the multiple time series design, draws upon the same logic but incorporates the advantage of a control group. Both the time series and multiple time series designs are based upon the assumption that observations are made at equal intervals. Diagramatically, the two designs can be illustrated as follows:

$$O_1 \ O_2 \ O_3 \ O_4 \ X \ O_5 \ O_6 \ O_7 \ O_8 \quad \text{(Time series)}$$

$$O_1 \ O_2 \ O_3 \ O_4 \ X \ O_5 \ O_6 \ O_7 \ O_8 \quad \text{(Multiple time series)}$$

$$O_1 \ O_2 \ O_3 \ O_4 \quad \ \ O_5 \ O_6 \ O_7 \ O_8$$

where O_1 through O_4 is the prechange period; X the change, intervention, or innovation; and O_5 through O_8 the postchange period. As Campbell and Julian C. Stanley note, the multiple time series design is "an excellent quasi-experimental design, perhaps the best of the more feasible designs" (1963, p. 57).[a]

That many public policy decisions can be investigated in the context of a time series design is apparent. For instance, this author has collaborated in an investigation of citizen reaction to annexation policies in which negative voting on budget measures was the periodic measurement, the annexed area the group, and the annexation the experimental change (Mushkatel, Wilson, and Mushkatel 1973). Among other examples of the use of this design are Gene V. Glass, George C. Tiao, and Thomas O. Maguire's examination of the impact of the revision of German divorce laws in 1900 upon the rates of divorce and petitions for divorce (1971); the effects of the British Road Safety Act of 1967 upon highway fatalities by H. Laurence Ross, Donald T. Campbell, and Gene V. Glass (1970); and the well known investigation of then Governor Ribicoff's crackdown on speeding by Campbell and Ross (1968). In addition, James R. Caporaso and Leslie L. Roos Jr. (1973) have recently edited a volume of papers dealing with both a discussion of quasi-

[a]Campbell and Stanley (1963) present an inventory of factors that jeopardize the internal and external validity of numerous research designs. The reader is directed to their discussion of these factors.

experimental methods and a number of examples of their application to the evaluation of public policies.

Unlike the more simple pretest—posttest design where a t test of mean difference might be appropriate, the interrupted time series design dictates the testing of difference of slopes and intercepts of regression estimates for the prechange and postchange periods. For instance, in this author's work cited above, interest was focused upon a change in negative voting subsequent to the experimental intervention—annexation. In this case, a change in slope would be represented by a progressively increasing or decreasing number of negative votes on budget measures over time. A change in intercept would take the form of an absolute increase, or decrease, in the number of negative votes over time.

Several statistics are available to test the impact of public policy when the research is cast in the quasi-experimental, interrrupted time series context. Each of these statistical tests is appropriate for a specifically formulated hypothesis. That is, some tests focus upon intercept differences and some upon differences in slope. For all tests, it is assumed that the change point is established independent of the data. However, if a researcher has sound theoretical reasons for expecting the treatment, innovation, or intervention to have a delayed impact, a number of postintervention observations may be included as prechange data points. Several tests should be considered here (Box and Tiao 1965, pp. 181-92; Mood 1950, pp. 297-98 and his double extrapolation technique, pp. 350-358; Walker and Lev 1953, three tests, pp. 390-95).

Mood Test

This test is appropriate for use by the investigator who wishes to know if the value of the first observation during a postchange period is significantly different than the value that would have been expected by a linear extrapolation of the prechange values. Although useful when one has a number of both prechange and postchange values, this test is particularly valuable when the investigator is confronted with but one postchange value and yet is desirous of making some inference about the impact of a specific policy upon a particular clientele or public.

More specifically, the Mood test incorporates the calculation of an expected first postchange value, based upon the regression equation of the prechange values, and then uses a t test of the significance of difference between this predicted value and the observed value.

Double Extrapolation Technique

This test approaches the measurement of significant differences between prechange and postchange observations in a manner somewhat similar to that of the Mood test. Whereas the Mood uses prechange values to predict a first postchange observation, the double extrapolation technique uses both prechange *and* postchange values to predict a y value at time t_0. This predicted y value lies midway between the last prechange point and the first postchange point. Unlike the Mood test, which tests the significance of differences between predicted and observed value, the double extrapolation technique tests the significance of difference between a value predicted for time t_0 by prechange values and one predicted for the same time t_0 by postchange values. This test is most appropriate when one has theoretical expectations that the slope of prechange and postchange values will be similar but the intercepts will be different.

Walker-Lev

Helen M. Walker and Joseph Lev have proposed three different tests of significant difference of slope that are appropriate for use in quasi-experimental designs. Each of these tests is based upon analysis of covariance and levels of significance are evaluated on the basis of F statistics.

The first of these is a test of the hypothesis of common slope for prechange and postchange periods. The second is a test of the hypothesis that the prechange and postchange slopes are equal to zero when $\hat{B}_1$ is found to equal $\hat{B}_2$. The third is a test of the hypothesis that a single regression line fits both prechange and postchange periods.

Clearly, for most research cast as quasi-experiments, the first and third tests of Walker and Lev are the most important. If the experimental change is intended to stimulate a new "trend" ($\hat{B}_1 \neq$

$\hat{B}_2$) as, for instance, a drug abuse prevention program, then the first test of Walker and Lev is most appropriate. If, on the other hand, the experimental change is intended to alter values for the postchange period by an increment or constant ($a_1 \neq a_2$) such as, for example, reducing welfare case loads by 10 percent, then one might use the third test of Walker and Lev.

Box and Tiao

G.E.P. Box and George C. Tiao have presented a statistic suitable for use in testing the significance of shifts in level of slope computed for prechange and postchange observations (that is, the significance of difference of intercepts). Their statistic is based upon an integrated moving average model that, simply stated, assumes that the system is subjected to periodic random shocks, a proportion of which are absorbed into the level of the series. As a result of these random shocks, it is expected that a plot of a time series will demonstrate a somewhat erratic pattern. Hence, the significance of an observed shift at a specified point is tested against the hypothesis that the shift is only that which would be expected by chance. Because this statistic assumes the time series will follow an erratic rather than linear pattern, this statistic should be given serious consideration in testing quasi-experimental, time series designs.[b]

Conclusion

The researcher who considers the use of these statistical models should be cautioned regarding several points. First, Joyce Sween and Donald T. Campbell (1965) have found that when a substantial amount of autocorrelation is present in one's data, the Mood, double extrapolation technique, and Walker-Lev statistics tend to indicate significant differences when, in fact, those differences are not significant. This seems to be a particular problem with the double extrapolation technique and the third test of Walker and Lev. Hence, when using these statistics, one should be careful of committing a Type II error, that is, rejecting the null hypothesis when it

---

[b]An excellent expansion upon the work begun by Box and Tiao (1965) is found in Gene V. Glass, Victor L. Willson, and John Mordechai Gottman (1972).

should be accepted. A close examination of a plot of the autocorrelations for several lags of the variable of interest should indicate the extent to which this source of error is present in one's data. Second, when using any of these statistics, the researcher should plot all of his observed values so as to investigate the possibility that the slope of the postchange values has its origin in the prechange period. Third, although mentioned earlier, it should be emphasized that the equality of intervals between observations is an important consideration in the use of the quasi-experimental time series design. Severe inequality of intervals between observations could, for instance, lead one to conclude that a significant change in the value of intercepts exists for prechange and postchange values when, in fact, no change occurred. Fourth, although the confidence a researcher can have in the results of his study will generally increase as the number of observations in both prechange and postchange periods increases, some tests are more sensitive than others to the number of observations in each period. For instance, the Mood test can be used when there is but one postchange value. The Walker-Lev statistics, on the other hand should probably be based upon a minimum of four observations in both prechange and postchange periods. Information presently available indicates that the Box and Tiao test requires substantially more observations in each period than the other tests but, as noted earlier, is less sensitive to assumptions of linearity.

Clearly, issues other than those touched upon in this review should be considered by the researcher who prepares to evaluate the impact of public policy through the use of the quasi-experimental, interrupted time series design. For instance, other authors have noted that one should be concerned with the consistency of reporting criteria of archival records (Campbell 1969), the adequacy of matching criteria when using the multiple time series design (Caporaso and Pelowski 1971), as well as other factors that jeopardize the internal and external validity of the designs (Campbell and Stanley 1963, pp. 40, 56). What should be emphasized, however, is that these designs and statistics for the testing of them are both appropriate and available for the evaluation of the impact of public policy.

Bibliography

Box, G.E.P., and George C. Tiao, June 1965. "A Change in Level of a Non-Stationary Time-Series," *Biometrika* 52, pp. 181-92.

Campbell, Donald T., 1967. "From Description to Experimentation: Interpreting Trends as Quasi-Experiments," in Chester W. Harris, ed., *Problems in Measuring Change* (Madison: The University of Wisconsin Press) pp. 212-42.

Campbell, Donald T., April 1969. "Reforms as Experiments," *American Psychologist* 24, pp. 409-29.

Campbell, Donald T., and H. Laurence Ross, January 1968. "The Connecticut Crackdown on Speeding: Time-Series Data in Quasi-Experimental Analysis," *Law and Society Review* 3, pp. 33-53.

Campbell, Donald T., and Julian C. Stanley, 1963. *Experimental and Quasi-Experimental Designs for Research* (Chicago: Rand McNally & Co.).

Caporaso, James A., and Alan L. Pelowski, June 1971. "Economic and Political Integration in Europe: A Time-Series Quasi-Experimental Analysis," *American Political Science Review* 65, pp. 418-33.

Caporaso, James A., and Leslie L. Roos, Jr., 1973. *Quasi-Experimental Approaches: Testing Theory and Evaluating Policy* (Evanston: Northwestern University Press).

Cook, Thomas J. and Frank P. Scioli, Jr., Autumn 1972. "Policy Analysis in Political Science: Trends and Issues in Empirical Research," *Policy Studies Journal* 1, pp. 6-11.

Fairweather, George W., 1967. *Methods for Experimental Social Innovation* (New York: John Wiley & Sons, Inc.).

Glass, Gene V., George C. Tiao, and Thomas O. Maguire, May 1971. "The 1900 Revision of German Divorce Laws: Analysis of Data as Time-Series Quasi-Experiment," *Law and Society Review* 6, pp. 339-62.

Glass, Gene V., Victor L. Willson, and John Mordechai Gottman, 1972. "Design and Analysis of Time-Series Experiments," mimeo, Laboratory of Educational Research, University of Colorado.

Mood, Alexander M., 1950. *Introduction to the Theory of Statistics* (New York: McGraw-Hill Book Co., Inc.).

Mushkatel, Alvin H., L.A. Wilson II, and Linda Mushkatel, December 1973. "A Model of Citizen Response to Annexation," *Urban Affairs Quarterly* 9, pp. 139-63.

Ross, H. Laurence, Donald T. Campbell, and Gene V. Glass, March/April 1970. "Determining the Social Effects of a Legal Reform," *American Behavioral Scientist* 13, pp. 493-509.

Sween, Joyce, and Donald T. Campbell, 1965. "A Study of the Effect of Proximally Autocorrelated Error on Tests of Significance for the Interrupted Time-Series Quasi-Experimental Design," mimeographed research report, Department of Psychology, Northwestern University.

Walker, Helen M., and Joseph Lev, 1953. *Statistical Inference* (New York: Holt, Rinehart and Winston).

11 Path Analytic Models in Policy Research

*Thomas R. Dye and
Neuman F. Pollack*

One of the acknowledged shortcomings of public policy research has been its failure to fully develop causal theory.[1] Most of the policy studies to date have relied primarily on associative reasoning and methodologies. Of course, exploring relationships between social, economic, and political variables and public policies is a necessary first step in the development of a policy science. But, increasingly, policy research will be concerned with the development of causal models—to better understand both the causes and consequences of public policies.

The utility of path analysis in policy research is its capacity to go beyond associative reasoning and to help clarify causal thinking.[2] Path analysis provides an opportunity to develop and test causal models which can help us to understand precisely *how* social, economic, or political forces go about shaping public policy, or precisely *how* public policies impact the social, economic, or political environment. It enables us (or compels us) to portray these ideas in diagrammatic fashion. Path analysis, like regression analysis, provides an overall estimate of the explanatory value of a model. Path analysis also assists in identifying spurious relationships. More importantly, it permits the testing of both direct and indirect causal paths in the determination of a dependent variable. We can ascertain whether a determining variable acts on a dependent variable directly, or through mediating variables, or both; and we can compare the relative influence of direct and indirect causal paths.

Path Analysis

Path analysis begins with the construction of diagramatic model in which *every* known determinant of a dependent variable is included

This chapter originally appeared in *Policy Studies Journal* 2 (Winter 1973), no. 2, pp. 123-30.

in the system. Causal paths are represented by arrows which connect the dependent variable with every independent variable, both directly and indirectly through mediating variables which are themselves completely determined. The dependent variable is generally placed at the far right of the diagram; variables which are not dependent upon any other variables in the system are placed at the far left; and the variables which help to determine the dependent variable but which themselves are determined by other variables in the system are placed in between.

In a study of policy *determinants,* where we are analyzing the causes of public policy, the policy itself would be placed at the far right of the diagram and the direct and indirect causal paths are traced back through intermediate variables to environmental conditions. In a study of policy *impacts*, where we are analyzing the consequences of public policy, the hypothesized impacts would be placed at the far right of the diagram and policy variables would be placed as intermediate variables, under the assumption that policies which impact some particular conditions are themselves shaped by other environmental conditions. This placement of policy variables in policy impact studies allows us to compare causal paths which flow *through* policy variables, with causal paths which proceed *directly* from environmental conditions to a presumed policy impact.

The placement of variables is a product of prior theoretical notions about the system. One must postulate time sequences, mechanisms of influence, and developmental processes in constructing a path analytic model. Knowledge of correlations is not enough. One must think about *how* variables might act on each other, and then construct a diagram which portrays these causal notions. The method of path analysis tests the notions which you have devised. But it cannot tell you what the true real-world system of relations are.

Variables at the far left of the diagram which are not determined by other variables in the system may themselves be intercorrelated. These unanalyzed correlations are shown by *curved* arrows, which call attention to the distinction between a correlation and a path relating a dependent to a determining variable.

In order to provide for the *complete* determination of the dependent variable and the mediating variables, it is necessary to introduce an array of residual or error terms indicating unexplained variance. These residual or error terms are represented by arrows in the same fashion as direct and indirect causal paths.

Path coefficients are estimated from a series of simultaneous regression equations in which first the dependent variable is regressed against all other variables as independent variables, and then mediating variables are treated sequentially as dependent variables with socioeconomic variables as independent variables. The path coefficients are standardized b values, or "beta coefficients"; these are obtained by multiplying the b value by the standard deviation of the independent variable divided by the standard deviation of the dependent variable. The paths from the residual values are calculated as $1 - R^2$, i.e., the square root of the unexplained variance in the multiple regression problems. The residual paths represent the effects of all unmeasured variables; but the adequacy of the model should not be judged by the size of the explained variance alone. It must also be judged by the accuracy of the relationships specified.

A causal path is eliminated from the hypothesized model if the *standard error* of any b value in any regression equation from a dependent variable to an independent variable is greater than the b value itself. The F statistic (analysis of variance) in such a case requires that the path be dropped from the causal model. The first series of simultaneous regression equations depicting the hypothesized model is only a first step: the primary purpose of these calculations is the elimination of paths which do not appear to make a significant contribution to variation in the dependent variable. A revised model with only influential paths represented is then calculated in a new series of regression equations. The revised model is simply the original model with paths erased where the corresponding b values turned out to be insignificant and negligible. In this new set of equations, the standardized b values, the "beta coefficients", become the *path coefficients*.

Assumptions

Assumptions of path analysis include the following: 1) that relationships are additive and linear, 2) that the residual "error" terms are uncorrelated, 3) that the causal paths involve no reciprocal causation, and 4) that the causal arrangement is appropriate. The first assumption is common in regression analysis; however, it should be noted that the presence of non-linear relationships may invalidate our conclusions. The second assumption is more troublesome. The only way of reducing the likelihood of outside error terms disturbing the equations is to bring into the model as explicit causal variables as many potentially disturbing influences as possible. The problem, of course, is that too many causal variables make the theoretical model unwieldy. Thus we must trade off possibilities of reaching erroneous conclusions against the value of achieving a reasonable clear and simple model. The third assumption is that we know the directions in which the causal arrows point, and that no causal arrow points in two directions simultaneously. In other words there must be no feedback loops occurring in the system. This assumption is also troublesome—particularly with regard to policy studies. One approach to this problem is to exercise care in time sequences between policy measures and environmental conditions. In a study of policy impacts, care must be exercised to insure that the policy measures are lagged in relation to their hypothesized impacts. In a study of policy determinants, care must be exercised to insure that policies occur after their presumed antecedents.

Finally, the causal model itself must be a theoretically satisfying one. Needless to say, there will always be a number of plausible alternative models which will yield approximately the same predictions as the model under study. We can only proceed by *eliminating* hypothesized but inadequate models. It is ordinarily impossible to rule out all of the logical alternative models. Thus, in a sense, one can never "establish" a particular causal model.

An Illustrative Model

Let us illustrate the uses of path analysis in a very simple exercise on the determinants of police protection in American cities. Variations in police protection are associated with a wide array of socioeconomic variables in American cities. Simple correlation coefficients based on 245 cities reveal that police manpower per 10,000 population is associated with size, income, race, and property-ownership, as well as crime rates and revenue levels.[a] But

---

[a]The simple correlation coefficients for relationships with policemen per 10,000 for 245 cities are: Population size: .36; nonwhite population percentage: .47; Percent Owner-occupied dwelling units: .48; Median family income: .13; crime rate: .48; Per capita total revenue: .57.

in order to explore causal relationships, some theoretical constructions are required.

Let us hypothesize that variations in police protection among
cities may be either a product of different *demands* for police protection, or different *resources* available to cities. Variables which may
affect *demands* include the size, income, racial, and property-
owning characteristics of a city's population. These socioeconomic
characteristics may create demands directly: for example, a large,
heavily non-white, non-property owning, low-income population
may create a demand for increased police protection. Or these same
socioeconomic characteristics may operate *indirectly* to create a
demand for police protection by affecting crime levels: A large,
heavily non-white, non-property owning, low-income population
may increase crime rates which *in turn* increase the demand for
police protection. Of course, size, income, occupation, race and
property-ownership also reflect a city's *resources* to provide any
public service. These variables may affect police expenditures
indirectly by affecting revenue levels which in turn enable a city to
provide increased police protection.

The model in Figure 11-1 represents these initial notions about
the possible direct and indirect determinant paths for urban police
protection. (We do not believe that increases in crime rates cause
increases in general revenue levels, or vice versa, even though these
variables are related. Hence, this linkage is missing from our causal
model.) Not all of these paths will prove to have a determining
impact on police protection. The broken line paths represent
hypothesized relationships which did not produce path coefficients
indicating significant causal effect.

The series of simultaneous regression equations presented in
Table 11-1 provide the calculations for determining the strength of
causal paths in our hypothesized model. The regression coefficients
(b values) and their standard errors are reported. Path coefficients
are shown for only those causal paths which proved to be influential.
In our model every path proved to be influential except two: from
population size to crime rates and from income to police manpower.

The model succeeds in explaining 68 percent of the total variance
in police expenditures among cities of 50,000 or more. As predicted,
crime rates and revenue levels were influential determinants of
police expenditures, suggesting the impact of both *demands* and
resources on spending for police protection. But environmental

Table 11-1
Regression Equations for Path Analytic Models for Police Protection

	Population	Income	Race	Homeowning	Crime	Revenue	R^2
Police Manpower							
b value	.16	.03	11.2	−10.6	10.3	.023	
s.e. of b	.05	.03	2.1	2.6	1.7	.004	.68
Path coef.	.11	a	.34	−.22	.15	.35	
Revenue							
b value	1.70	1.39	86.5	−420			
s.e. of b	.84	.40	36.0	38			.42
Path coef.	.11	.18	.13	−.57			
Crime Rate							
b value	.00	.002	.47	−.40			
s.e. of b	.00	.001	.07	−.08			.30
Path coef.	a	.13	.37	−.29			

aPath eliminated, not significant

variables—size, income, race and home ownership—also operated directly on police expenditures as well as *indirectly* through crime rates and revenue levels.

Race is the most influential environmental variable in the *demand* path to police protection. Race affects police expenditures *directly*: an increase in non-white populations percentage is associated with an increase in police manpower. And race also affects police expenditures *indirectly*: an increase in non-white population percentage is associated with an increase in crime rates which is in turn associated with an increase in police manpower.

Home ownership is the most influential environmental variable in the *resource* path to police expenditures. Home ownership affects police expenditures *directly*: an increase in home ownership is associated with a decrease in police protection. Home ownership also affects police protection *indirectly* by reducing municipal revenue levels which in turn affect police manpower. Home ownership is also influential in the *demand* path, although not *as* influential as race. Home ownership reduces the demand for police protection by reducing crime rates.

Size and *income* also contribute to the explanation of police protection, although their influence is not as great as race and home ownership. Size does not appear to affect crime rates (at least not variations in city size among cities over 50,000). But increases in size

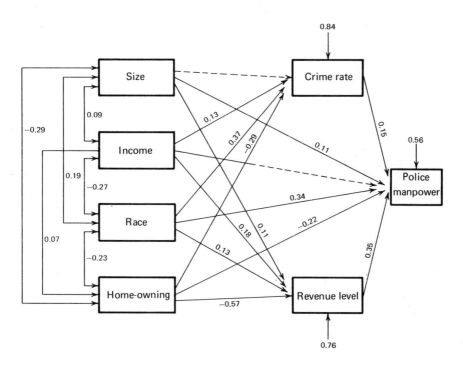

Figure 11-1. Path Analysis: Police Manpower

are modestly associated with increases in revenue levels and increases in police manpower. Income is positively associated with crime rates, and revenue levels, but there is no direct path from income to police protection, suggesting that income affects police protection only *indirectly* through increasing both crime and revenue levels.

Generally the *direct* path of the environmental variables are stronger than the *indirect* paths through either crime rates or revenue levels. This is largely a product of the fact that the environmental variables explain less than half of the variation in crime rates and revenue levels. Since the environmental variables fail to account for half of the variation in these mediating factors, the influence of environmental forces *through* these factors is weakened. Nonetheless, both the demand (crime rate) path and resource (revenue level) path are confirmed by the coefficients. The path of property ownership through revenue levels to police expenditures is the strongest of the indirect paths.

Perhaps the most noteworthy finding of this brief path analytic exercise is that police manpower increase as a *direct* result of non-white populations increases, regardless of the effect of these increases on the crime rate! There is no question that black population increases affect crime rates; this finding has been reported frequently.[3] But path analysis suggests that black population increases produce increased police expenditures and police manpower *beyond* the increases coming about through increased crime rates. It is doubtful that blacks themselves are demanding these increases in police manpower. (Correlations among aggregate populations do not permit inferences about individual behavior.) We are tempted to speculate that *white* populations demand increased police protection when black population percentages increase—that *they demand more police protection than required to cope with the increased crime rates.*

Path Analysis in Policy Research

As policy research becomes increasingly theory-oriented, it will require increasingly complex causal models and appropriate methodologies for testing these models. Our brief exercise suggests the way in which path analysis can be employed to better understand policy *determination*. But path analysis also provides a useful technique in studies of policy *impact*. Policy measures can be portrayed as mediating variables in causal models, and path coefficients can allow us to compare the direct effects of environmental variables on societal changes, with the indirect effects flowing through policy measures. In general, path analysis is a more powerful tool in causal modeling than earlier Simon-Blalock techniques. Of course, no methodology substitutes for thinking about what is happening in the real world.

Notes

1. Robert Salisbury, "The Analysis of Public Policy: The Search for Theories and Roles" in Austin Ranney (ed.) *Political Science and Public Policy* (Chicago: Markham, 1968), 151-178. See also Ira

Sharkansky (ed.), *Policy Analysis in Political Science* (Chicago: Markham, 1970).

2. Path analysis is by no means a new methodology. Sewall Wright published the first article on the topic in 1921, and the method was discussed at length in biology and genetics in the 1920s and 30s. Sewall Wright, "Correlation and Causation", *Journal of Agricultural Research* Vol. 20 (1921), 557-585; H. E. Niles, "Correlation, Causation, and Wright's Theory of 'Path Coefficients'," *Genetics* Vol. 7 (1922), 258-273; Sewall Wright, "The Theory of Path Coefficients: A Reply to Niles's Criticism," *Genetics* Vol. 8 (1923), 239-255; H. E. Niles, "The Method of Path Coefficients: An Answer to Wright," *Genetics* Vol. 8 (1923) 256-260; Sewall Wright, "The Method of Path Coefficients" *Annals of Mathematical Statistics* Vol. 5 (1934), 161-215; J. W. Tukey, "Causation, Regression and Path Analysis," in Oscar Kempthorne (ed.), *Statistics and Mathematics in Biology* (New York: Hafner Publishing Co., 1954); Sewall Wright, "Path Coefficients and Path Regressions: Alternative or Complementary Concepts", *Biometrics* Vol. 16 (1960), 180-202; Malcolm E. Turner and Charles D. Stevens, "The Regression Analysis of Causal Paths," *Biometrics* Vol. 15 (1959), 236-258. Econometricians developed an extensive literature in path analysis and related techniques in the 1950s. See E. Malinvaud, *Statistical Methods of Econometrics* (Chicago: Rand McNally, 1966). Raymond Boudon recommended path analysis to sociologists in 1965 as an improvement over the Simon-Blalock type of causal modeling, which Boudon labeled as a "weak form" of path analysis. (Boudon referred to path analysis as "dependence analysis", but "path analysis" seems to be the more common usage.) Raymond Boudon, "A Method of Linear Causal Analysis: Dependence Analysis", *American Sociological Review* Vol. 30 (June, 1965); 365-374. See also Hubert M. Blalock Jr., *Causal Inferences in Nonexperimental Research* (Chapel Hill: University of North Carolina Press, 1964). Otis Dudley Duncan also recommended this technique to sociologists as "useful in making explicit the rationale of conventional regression equations"; he re-analyzed data from several sociological studies to demonstrate the utility of the method. Otis Dudley Duncan, "Path Analysis: Sociological Examples," *American Journal of Sociology* Vol. 72 (July, 1966), 1-16. In 1967 H. M. Blalock, Jr. discussed the utility of closed theoretical systems in

causal inference (and hence by implication the utility of path analysis) in political science—specifically in the study of constituency influence in congressional voting behavior. H. M. Blalock, Jr., "Causal Inferences, Closed Populations, and Measures of Association," *American Political Science Review* Vol. 61 (March, 1967), 130-136. Yet policy research, in political science at least, has not yet moved beyond the Simon-Blalock technique. See Charles F. Cnudde and Donald J. McCrone, "Party Competition and Welfare Policies in the American States," *American Political Science Review* Vol. 63 (September, 1969), 858-866. Nonetheless, it is very likely that path analysis will be employed increasingly as policy researchers seek to develop and test increasingly complex causal models. See also H. M. Blalock, Jr. (ed.), *Causal Models in the Social Sciences* (New York: Aldine-Atherton, 1971).

3. See E. Terrence Jones, "Evaluating Everyday Policies: Police Activity and Crime Incidence", *Urban Affairs Quarterly* (March, 1973), 267-279.

12 A Methodological Problem in the Socio-Economic Interpretation of State Spending

James W. Dyson and
Douglas St. Angelo

One principle line of interpretation from policy outputs analysis is that taxing and spending policies are largely determined by the socio-economic environment.[1] The broad implications of the socio-economic interpretation—which simultaneously emphasizes environmental determinants and de-emphasizes political factors —demand a serious evaluation of the methodology on which the interpretation is based. Before we fully accept this view of policy making, we must be certain that the environment is a main *determinant* of outputs.

From a methodological point of view the socio-economic interpretation involves quantitative analysis, most particularly correlational analysis. What we question in this paper is the suitability of the correlational statistic (Pearson's r)—or, in this context, the companion regression statistic—as applied to situations involving changes in the unit of observation as a basis for measuring changes in Environmental-Spending relationships.

Typically, policy research compares selected political variables and the socio-economic environment of the american states with state spending policies at one point in time. Consequently, a crucial assumption is made, to wit: if some wealthy states are high spenders, some less wealthy states are average spenders, and some poor states are low spenders, the socio-economic environment influences spending policies. This line of reasoning is so intuitively satisfying, it is seldom questioned. This is somewhat surprising on two counts. First, the evidence presented does not suggest that the pattern of association is pervasive. Second, the argument itself is not indubitable. Since the evidence we are referring to has been presented in the policy research literature (see Reference 1), we will turn to the argument.

This chapter originally appeared in *Policy Studies Journal* 2 (Winter 1973), no. 2, pp. 131-36.

It is our position that the environmental argument essentially holds that spending policies are largely determined by a state's socio-economic environment. If this is so, then changes in this environment should be accompanied by systematic spending changes. In any antecedent relationship, a change in the antecedent leads to a change in that which it determines. An antecedent relationship is distinguishable from a co-variation relationship. If two variables merely *co-vary to a small* degree, then changes in one will not be systematically followed by changes in the other. The changes would be jointly occurring *only if* the variables were directly linked together and the associations were strong. If the variables were not directly linked together there would be a lag between the changes in one and the changes in the other. If the association were weak only some changes in one variable would be accompanied by changes in the other variable.[2]

It is obvious that there is a considerable difference between an argument about an antecedent relationship and an argument about a co-varying relationship. But one facet of the difference we have paid for too little attention to concerns the issue of explanation. In a determinate relationship, the antecedent explains the occurrence of the other variable. In a co-variation relationship, the explanation is not at hand. That is, whether the variables are linked directly and what factors lead them to co-vary are not known. In other words, there is co-incidental occurrence, but no explanation.[3]

Unless one is analyzing results obtained in a controlled experiment, neither correlational nor regression statistics allow a deterministic interpretation. One way to deal with this problem, outside of an experimental situation, is to study whether the actual changes in one variable set bear a substantial relationship to changes in the other variable set. Stated in terms of the environment-spending argument, the question is: Do states change their spending policies as their socio-economic environment changes? If the relationship is antecedent or direct, the spending policies of states will respond to environmental changes. If the association is merely a weak, co-varying relationship, the changes will not be closely associated.[4]

The above reasoning led us to take the differences between observations made at two points in time for each state on all variables. Per capita personal income in 1960, for example, was compared with per capita personal income in 1967 to obtain a difference score. This difference score represents the change in per capita personal income. The same procedure was used with all of the environmental and spending variables reported in the policy outputs literature. If these changes are not highly correlated, the associations between the variables are not direct and, therefore, the relationship is not an antecedent one. The matter of what leads states to vary their spending policies would remain largely unanswered. Moreover, we would not actually know what links the environment to spending. If the relationship is not antecedent or directly co-varying, the co-incidental association between the environment and spending is of small consequence in the attempt to explain state spending policies.

Data Analysis

The first step we took in analyzing the data, while being consistent with the above discussion, was to evaluate the relationships obtaining between the environmental variables and the policy variables at two points in time independently.[a]

Persistent relationships were found between (1) industrialization with outputs, which was negative or inversely related, and (2) per capita personal income with outputs. Thus, only personal income acted in the expected fashion. In both 1960 and 1967, this independent variable retained a reasonably high, positive relationship with a goodly proportion of the output variables. Moreover, it related to some of the same dependent variables at both points in time. This means that the patterns of relationships meet a standard of consistency. It is necessary to maintain consistent patterns in relationships over time because co-varying relationships must be persistent if one is to argue the variable sets are indeed associated.

Although per capita personal income maintained a consistent relationship with policy variables there are indications of a lack of stability in the associations. The magnitude of the correlations ob-

---

[a]The large number of variables used in relating the environment to spending policies may be found in sources included in Reference 1. A fuller discussion of spending variables may be found in Thomas R. Dye, "Malapportionment and Public Policy in the States," *Journal of Politics,* vol. 27, August, 1965.

The data set compiled for this study included all the variables reported in the literature. The collection and analysis of the data was made possible by a grant to the Political Research Institute, Florida State University, from Contract #OEg-4-9-190746-0014-095 from the Department of Health, Education and Welfare. The sources of the data were: *Statistical Abstract of the United States,* U. S. Department of Commerce, Bureau of the Census, 1961 and 1968.

tained with the 1960 data differed substantially from those obtained with the 1967 data. Since the two income variables are highly inter-correlated (1972), the differences obtained in two of the four persistent relationships are about as large as one may expect to obtain given their intercorrelations. The two income variables *only fail* to share about 05.5 percent of their variation, yet in relation to outputs the two variables are differentially associated by as much as 15 percent. Theoretically, the magnitude of the relationships between each of the income variables with the policy variables would be approximately the same if the joint distributions were stable over time.[b] The instability between these relationships is another indication of the need to correlate difference scores in the attempt to determine the type of relationship existing between income and spending policies.

The change in the degree of association indicates instability in the co-varying relationships. When variables co-vary differently at different points in time their connection is either spurious or controlled by an exogenous lag factor. If a lag factor is functioning, then the correlation between difference scores should be high. The principle of the differential in calculus suggest that for any curve involving slope the change in one of the variables is a function of the change in the independent variable.[5] If this is not the case the interpretation of the association between the actual observations is simply unclear.[6]

In correlating change there was a definite dearth of correlation above .40.[c] (See Table 12-1.) Thus, changes in the environment are infrequently related to changes in outputs. In the data sets used here not one of the changes correlated above .40 which indicated gross instability. The unrelatedness of environmental changes and output changes indicates that the static but persistent relationship of industrialization and per capita personal income with the dependent variables is not reflecting a causal or functional relationship. Simply put, correlations like the ones discussed above merely indicate that a state's position on one dimension *is occasionally too frequently congruent* with that state's position on the other dimension as long as the amount of change in the variable sets is ignored.

---

[b]Although the procedure employed here is somewhat analogous to time-series analysis, the two methods differ in a number of respects. The most important difference is that with time-series analysis one must use a number of data points. Reference 6 refers to economic literature which uses procedures like those used here.

[c].40 is a satisfactory minimal level because it is the minimum correlation insuring us that at least 10 percent of the variation in the independent variable relates to the variation in the dependent variable.

Table 12-1
Change in Environment in Relation to Change in Outputs

Change in Outputs	Population Density	% Change Urban	Per Capita Personal Income	Industrialization
State and Local				
General Expenditures	.06	−.03	.35	−.18
General Expenditures, Education	.09	.15	.20	−.06
State Only				
Expenditures, Per Pupil in ADA	.16	.21	.26	−.11
Expenditures, Welfare	.19	.17	.29	−.10
Expenditures, Health & Hospitals	.09	−.06	.31	−.12

The overall pattern of results does not even encourage using environmental variable as predictor criteria to evaluate next year's spending. Sharkansky's incremental position would be more helpful in predicting future spending.[7] If his view were modified to include revenue variables to estimate spending, it might even be feasible to predict spending immediately after a change in a tax structure. This may be accomplished by estimating revenues the new structure would produce and allocating available funds on the basis of proportionate allotments that were used in the past. For the two years we have studied the change in state and local revenues is highly correlated with the change in general expenditures of state and local governments (.934), so there may be a real possibility of using a modified version of incrementalism to predict future spending. But only prediction would be involved as the variation in relationship of counterpart variables indicates that a routine decision in one state is not always the same in another state.[d] This lack of a clear decisional

---

[d]In one sense this view merely suggests that the more a state has the more a state spends, but the important point to consider is whether larger amounts of available monies are disbursed on the basis of existing allotment ratios. If so, the incremental model would show that increases in spending were a function of prior spending ratios.

pattern places severe restrictions on an incremental interpretation of taxing and spending policies.

Conclusions

The data presented here suggest that there may be no real basis for asserting that taxing and spending policies are a *function* of a state's socio-economic environment. A change in the environment of less privileged states may not lead to comprehensible changes in relative levels of spending. At the very least, decision making conversion and cultural milieu influence the translation of environmental changes into policies in significant ways. Although this analysis cannot shed light on the conversion process, we may gain some comfort, and prodding towards future research, from knowing that hard evidence supporting the environmental deterministic argument is unavailable. Decision makers so influence how environmental changes are translated into taxing and spending policies that the average change in the independent variables are seldomly accompanied by successive changes in the dependent variables. In no case did the environment definitely account for 10 percent of the variance in spending. Concomitantly, some states are able to change their position on spending without a positional change in their relative ranking on socio-economic variables. Yet let us be clear that this analysis in no way suggests that environment and spending do not commingle. What the analysis suggests is that we must begin to learn what set of variables commingles them, if we wish to enlarge our understanding of policy making.

Notes

1. Findings supporting the economic-environmental deterministic position can be found in the following works: Richard E. Dawson and James A. Robinson, "Inter-Party Competition, Economic Variables and Welfare Policies in the American States." *The Journal of Politics*, XXV, (May, 1963), 265-289. Thomas R. Dye, *Politics, Economics and the Public: Policy Outcomes in the American States*, (Chicago: Rand McNally & Co., 1969). Thomas R. Dye, "Malapportionment and Public Policy in the States," *The Journal of*

Politics, XXVII, (August, 1965), 586-601. Thomas R. Dye, "Governmental Structure, Urban Environment, and Educational Policy," *Midwest Journal of Political Science,* XL (August, 1967), 353-380. Richard I. Hofferbert, "The Relation between the American States," *The American Political Science Review,* LX, (March, 1966), 73-82. To simplify technology this group will be referred to as economic determinists in this report.

2. See F. A. Grayhill, *An Introduction to Linear Statistical Models,* (New York: McGraw-Hill Book Company, 1968), Vol. 1; J. P. Guilford, *Fundamental Statistics in Psychology and Education,* chapter 61; William Mendenhall, *Introduction to Linear Models and the Design and Analysis of Experiments,* (Belmont, Colorado: Wadsworth, 1968), especially chapter 3.

3. E. Nagel, *The Structure of Science,* (New York: Harcourt, Brace and World, 1961), 73-78. In this section Nagel distinguishes between dynamical laws (function in time) and causal laws and points out how respectable time is as an independent variable.

4. See, for example, James S. Coleman, "The Mathematical Study of Change," in Hubert M. and Ann B. Blalock (editors), *Methodology in Social Research.* (New York: McGraw-Hill Book Company, 1968).

5. See, for example, Howard E. Taylor and Thomas L. Wade, *University Calculus,* (New York: John Wiley & Sons), especially pp. 93-102 and 147-176.

6. Cross-lagging is another technique political scientists might develop to study environmental-policy relationships, especially if one specifies intervening mechanisms between the independent and dependent variables. See, for example, William D. Crano, David A. Kenny and Donald T. Campbell, "Does Intelligence Cause Achievement?: a Cross-Lagged Panel Analysis," *Journal of Educational Psychology,* 1972, Vol. 63, No. 3, 268-275; Richard M. Rozelle and Donald T. Campbell, "More Plausible Rival Hypotheses in the Cross-Lagged Panel Correlation Technique," *Psychological Bulletin,* 1969, Vol. 71, No. 1, 74-80; for a general treatment of the approach used in this paper see P. Rao & R. Miller, *Applied Econometrics,* (Belmont, Calif.:, 1972).

7. Ira Sharkansky, *The Politics of Taxing and Spending,* (Indianapolis: Bobbs-Merrill, 1969); for the general utility of incrementalism in this context see O. A. Davis, M. A. H. Dempster and A. W.

Wildavsky, "A Theory of the Budgetary Process," *American Political Science Review,* September, 1966.

13

The Economic Evaluation of Policy Impacts: Cost-Benefit and Cost-Effectiveness Analysis

Ronald W. Johnson and John M. Pierce

The terms cost-benefit, cost-effectiveness, cost-utility, and systems analysis often have been used interchangeably.[1] The indiscriminate use of these terms has been confusing especially to the administrator or student who is trying to understand the various techniques and tools available for program evaluation. For purposes of this chapter, it is important to distinguish among these terms and to place cost-benefit and cost-effectiveness within the more macroframework of system analysis. In general terms, *systems analysis* can be conceptualized as an analytical technique used for scanning and identifying the work outputs that are most effective for accomplishing particular design objectives. In this macro-type approach there are five distinct functions.[2] Although there is a certain amount of overlap among the functions, essentially they are performed sequentially. Table 13-1 summarizes these five functions in outline form.

First a careful specification of program objectives must be made. Until the program objectives—the values of the system being considered—are specified, the program does not take on meaning and it is not possible to determine what the program is to accomplish. Program objectives are stated in terms of measurable program accomplishments—impacts. These impact measures are specified in terms of the characteristics of human behavior or the environment to be changed or affected by the program being evaluated. Work output or the quantifiable units produced by governmental activities that can be identified as having a causal relationship to impact measures must be determined. Only after the precise statement of program objectives in terms of impact measures and work outputs has been made is it possible to evaluate program success or failure.

Second, it is necessary to search for and select alternative ways or combinations of work output for accomplishing the stated program objectives. This is obviously an important aspect of program

Table 13-1
Steps in Systems Analysis

1. Specification of design or program objectives
2. Selection of alternative means of accomplishing program objectives
3. Measurement of costs and benefits or results of each alternative
4. Comparison of alternatives
5. Presentation of relevant choices

evaluation in that "although the wise (optimum) choice depends on good judgment—good and relevant alternatives must be present."[3]

Third, it is necessary to measure the costs and benefits or results of each alternative over the period during which the program is realistically expected to have effect. Choice of the relevant time horizon usually is dependent on the expected life span of the program or project, and measurement of cost is usually in terms of dollars. While results often are stated in terms of dollars, in many cases it is necessary to state the measurement of effectiveness in nondollar terms, such as number of lives saved.

The fourth step involves a comparison of alternatives. Because in the public sector one is dealing with a budget constraint, comparisons ideally are made in dollar terms. Program alternatives that each have different measures of effectiveness essentially are impossible to compare. For example, how does one compare a reduction in the incidence of mortality from cancer with better education achieved by minorities through preschool head-start programs? When dollar quantification of results is not possible, the analyst is restricted to comparing alternatives with the same measures of effectiveness or to assessing the cost of a single policy or alternative in comparison with the benefits thereof.

In comparison of alternatives, the fifth step, presentation, is involved. Pure cost and/or benefit data must be translated into meaningful terms understandable to the decision maker. Qualifying assumptions, limitations, and constraints must be stated explicitly in order to give the decision maker a complete assessment of his alternatives.

Of the above five basic steps involved in systems or program analysis, cost-benefit and cost-effectiveness analyses are concerned primarily with the last three. It should be stressed that cost-benefit and cost-effectiveness analysis are not synonymous with systems analysis. Generally, the cost-benefit or cost-effectiveness analyst is given both the program objectives and the relevant alternatives to be considered. Failure to state program objectives for the analyst places him in a policy-making position thus usurping the function of the person requesting the analysis. Although in the process of analysis new objectives and alternatives may surface and may be presented to the decision maker along with original constraints, most cost-benefit and cost-effectiveness studies begin with a constrained set of objectives and alternatives that are the result of political, economic, or social considerations.

Cost-benefit analysis should be distinguished from cost-effectiveness analysis. Both costs and benefits are measured in terms of dollars in cost-benefit analysis whereas in cost-effectiveness analysis, benefits are not stated in dollar terms. Historically, cost-effectiveness studies have been applied most often to military weapon systems where results might be measured in such terms as bomb tonnage delivered or strike force capacity. Cost-benefit studies, on the other hand, have been applied most successfully to long-range capital investments such as public water resource projects where the dollar returns are more susceptible to measurement. Cost-effectiveness analysis is most frequently used in situations where the level of accomplishment is stated in terms of minimum acceptable levels, and the object is to find the least cost combination of ways of accomplishing or satisfying the stated objectives.[4] In cost-benefit studies, neither costs nor benefits are fixed at a given level but rather are variable. Otherwise, the two analytical techniques are essentially the same, especially with respect to the measurement of costs.

The following discussion of the methods and limitations of cost-benefit and cost-effectiveness analysis is divided into four sections. First is a general discussion of both analytical techniques and the context of their theoretical and methodological traditions. This section is a necessary prelude to developing a critical awareness of the assumptions and limitations of the techniques. The second section considers the relevant costs that should be considered in both types of analysis. The third section develops the concept of measurement of results, either benefits in terms of dollars or nondollar measures of effectiveness. In the fourth section, special problems in the application of both techniques are discussed. At the conclusion, the student and the administrator are assured that the analytical techniques discussed in this chapter may be applied to problems ranging from the simple to the complex, that the methodology of cost-benefit and cost-effectiveness analysis is within the scope of most academic policy analysis concerns and the needs of administrators for usable program evaluation techniques.

Behavior Maximization

Both cost-benefit and cost-effectiveness analysis are analytical tools that fit within the general theory of behavior maximization.[5] That is, both are techniques intended to provide information contributing to the attainment of maximum system performance. As such, both are narrower than systems analysis in that they include or are concerned with only part of the systems analysis model presented in the introduction.

In the private sector the ultimate measure of system performance to be maximized is profits. Programs and program alternatives are measured in terms of profits generated. The optimum program size is determined when profits are greatest given the constraints of fixed variables. In the private sector, production of a particular product, given profit maximization, should continue to increase as long as the incremental or marginal revenue exceeds the incremental cost for each additional unit of production. Further, the concept of profit makes it possible through a market mechanism to determine what should and what should not be produced in terms of social demand. In the public sector, however, there is no market mechanism that acts as a regulator and provides information concerning what should be produced and whether there is too little or too much of a given product. In the economic sense, no market mechanism such as profit exists that indicates when marginal cost equals marginal revenue, thus indicating optimum program size. No market mechanism exists in the public sector that allows recipients or clients of a public sector service to signal through their consumer behavior whether the service is adequate, whether it is economically feasible, or whether it could be provided at a lower cost. Cost-benefit and cost-effectiveness analyses, or systems analysis more generally, are an attempt to provide information comparable to the private sector's calculations of profit.

A single program alternative, several alternatives within the same program, or several different programs involving different governmental functions may be subjected to cost-benefit or cost-effectiveness analyses in which the objective is to maximize governmental performance. Cost-benefit and cost-effectiveness analysis, or economic analysis, within the broader framework of program evaluation, have three interrelated functions that correspond to the three related levels of program mix that can be used. First is a comparison of programs that are competing for the same resources. In economic analyses, only programs with similar objectives are normally compared. Generally comparison of widely different programs, such as police protection versus health, is a policy level function. That is, the determination of which substantive program area should be enacted is a question of priorities and not one of economic analysis. It is a political rather than an economic question.

The second function is the evaluation of alternative ways for achieving given program objectives, such as alternative disease control proposals. Third is making calculations for the various alternatives so that optimal program size can be determined. That is, at what point do additional expenditures cease contributing to further accomplishment of program objectives. To the extent that both costs and benefits can be measured in dollar terms, cost-benefit analysis may be used to aid in the efficient allocation of resources among alternative substantive programs. However, because most programs carry with them a decision rule dealing with distribution, the traditional economic efficiency criterion is not sufficient for decision making. When the measurement of objectives is in non-monetary terms, analysis is limited to the marginal analysis of alternative means of achieving given program objectives. The latter is the primary domain of cost-effectiveness analysis. This does not mean that cost-benefit analysis is used for comparing alternative substantive programs and cost-effectiveness analysis is used for functions two and three described above, but rather it means that cost-benefit can be used only in those areas in which benefits can realistically be specified in dollar terms. The only time in which economic analysis can be used for the comparison of programs competing for the same resources is when those substantive areas are closely related and also have some mechanism that can specify a common denominator for determining impact measures.

While some persons argue that the use of cost-benefit analysis might lead to the elimination of an entire substantive area of service—perhaps defense or social security—in order to be efficient economically, political and social constraints usually specify minimum levels of service regardless of the cost. With governmental objectives being specified by the policy makers in most cases, the analytical problem becomes one of minimizing costs subject to some politically specified level of effectiveness or maximizing effectiveness subject to a budget constraint. As should be evident, cost-benefit analysis is more applicable to capital investment projects such as sewage treatment plants or water resource development, whereas cost-effectivness analysis is most useful in some of the "softer" human service areas or in services such as defense that are not concerned with monetary type results.

Historically, cost-effectiveness analysis was developed at the federal government level in the Department of Defense and has received most of its publicity in relationship to the development of alternative weapons systems. In military usage, the first step is the determination of enemy intentions and capabilities. Given this information, United States desired capabilities are then determined. These capabilities are then translated into requirements that are stated in terms of developing a bomb with a given megatonnage and given method of delivery, one that can be stored for a definite period and is relatively safe from any enemy first attack, and so forth. When all the requirements are specified, the cost-effectivness problem is to find the best way to meet them. This may mean the best single program or the best mix of programs.

As can be seen, the rationale for cost-effectiveness differs somewhat from that for cost-benefit analysis where the attempt is to show a positive relationship between cost and benefits, both stated in dollar terms. In a way, the cost-benefit problem is more complicated than is the cost-effectiveness one in that in cost-benefit it is necessary to be able to state both costs and benefits in terms of a common denominator. The cost side of this problem is normally much less difficult than is the problem of valuing benefits in dollar terms. In the case of cost-effectiveness, the benefit side has been simplified somewhat in that it is not necessary to state benefits in terms of dollars.

Cost-effectiveness has been referred to most often as being applicable primarily in the area of national security where one can say "we do not want to spend any more than we have to, but we will spend all we have to to accomplish the stated objectives." While this situation occurs in the area of defense, there are many other substantive areas in which it is now believed that certain objectives or requirements will have to be met within a given time frame if the system is going to survive. Given these system survival requirements, policy decisions will have to be made stating some level of accomplishment that must be achieved. Once the political decision has been made, the problem becomes one of how to achieve most effectively these objectives. The question is not one of balancing benefits against costs, for the benefits have already been politically determined to be necessary, and in these nonnational security areas the statement still is "we do not want to spend any more than we have to, but we will spend all we have to."

In the use of cost-benefit analysis, the importance has been stressed of being able to compare benefits with costs to determine if the project will produce a social "profit." Underlying this idea is the assumption that all meaningful social benefits can be determined, assessed, and reduced to a single numerical value. However, with many traditional government social programs, many of the social benefits are not subject to being expressed in common monetary terms. This is especially true where such things as life and death, health, domestic security, and income distribution are included in the analysis. The attempt to state benefits and cost in dollar terms is based on the belief that the economic analysis criterion of efficiency is valid and will be relied on in making political decisions. Public policy decisions, however, are normally not economically relevant in terms of "profits" as that term is loosely used in economics, but rather decisions are inclined to be qualitatively relevant from the point of view of systems survival as viewed from the perspective of the decision maker. For capital investment projects, where the results may more easily be expressed in monetary terms, cost-benefit analysis should be helpful. For example, while the decision as to whether or not to have a sewage treatment plant is normally not one of the alternatives, several types of sewage treatment facilities may be evaluated in terms of economic costs and benefits.

Cost Measurement

There are two concepts of cost relevant to both cost-benefit and cost-effectiveness analysis—economic costs and budget costs.

Budget costs are the monetary values of the resources used in conducting a program or providing a service. These are the costs normally associated with the budget document, and they measure the extent of actual governmental outlay necessary to conduct a project. Little argument needs to be given for counting budget costs as relevant costs in an economic analysis of program impacts; there are, however, some problems of budget costs measurement that will be considered below. The concept of economic costs, on the other hand, presents considerably more difficulties. Basic to the notion of economic costs is the concept of opportunity costs—the value of opportunities foregone. The diversion of resources from the private sector to the public sector means that those resources are no longer available for private consumptive purposes. The value of these private consumptive purposes is therefore the economic cost to the government of its programs. The allocation of funds among programs within the public sector also means that other competing public uses for these funds are not served. The cost of a particular project, therefore, is the value of other public sector projects that otherwise could have been funded. These economic or opportunity costs may be equal to or greater than, but never less than, the budget costs.

Economic Costs

Whereas budget costs are direct monetary costs to government, economic cost is a more inclusive concept that demands the consideration of costs regardless of where they fall. The dollar costs of a public project are considered as direct cost to taxpayers. However, many government projects may involve spillover costs (and benefits which will be considered in the next section). These spillover costs are referred to as externalities. Externalities refer to the incidence of the impact. This means the unit that bears the extra cost or benefit, regardless of the form the cost takes, is managerially independent of the unit deciding on the particular course of action which caused or created the externalities.

Externalities involve two distinguishing characteristics: (1) interdependence, and (2) proper compensation is not paid. Symbolically externalities can be represented as follows:

$$U^A = U^A (X_1, \ldots, X_n, Y_1, Y_2, \ldots, Y_n)$$

The utility (U) of the autonomous unit (A) is dependent on activities $(X_1, X_2, \ldots, X_n)$, which are exclusively under its own control, but also the U^A is dependent on one or more activities $(Y_1, Y_2, \ldots, Y_n)$, which are, by definition, under control of one or more other autonomous decision-making units. Further, the positive and negative effect on U^A by activities $(Y_1, Y_2, \ldots, Y_n)$ are not compensated for in any manner by the entity receiving the benefit or causing the damage. Or, Municipality A controls its own water and sewer treatment facilities (activities $X_1, X_2, \ldots, X_n$) but it has no control over Municipality B's sewage treatment facility (activity Y_1) which is located upstream. Because Municipality B does not have secondary treatment facilities, Municipality A pays higher cost for its own water treatment. This higher cost is outside A's control and is uncompensated. Thus, it is an externality caused by B.

A. R. Prest and R. Turvey in their survey of cost-benefit analysis provide another example of external diseconomies imposed on one government service through the improvement of another service: "Construction of a fast motorway, which in itself speeds up traffic and reduces accidents, may lead to more congestion or more accidents on feeder roads if they are left unimproved."[6] The construction of a government funded dam not only involves the direct expenditure of public funds but it may also impose costs on private parties and public jurisdictions. Private parties may lose land, may have their land values lowered, or may have to relocate places of business, and municipal water supplies may be affected adversely. All of these constitute relevant economic costs of the dam project. To the extent that private or public organizations find their positions enhanced by the dam, the costs are negative costs, or benefits.

A different kind of cost often not considered relevant to the evaluation of program impacts in economic analysis is that of a program's redistributive effects. For policies explicitly designed to redistribute income, for example social security, the redistributive effects are naturally the principal focus. For other programs, however, the redistributive effects often are ignored or at best casually regarded. For example, a scholarship program for special classes of people has a long-run redistributive effect enhancing those special classes relative to other classes. Lax enforcement of a regulatory policy provides benefits for those supposedly regulated while at the same time imposes costs on the general public such as allowing unsafe drugs to be produced or allowing substandard food products to reach the public. The lax enforcement redistributes what would be the costs of complying with regulations from those being regulated to the general public. Although the difficulties involved may be great in trying to determine and measure what the relevant redistributive effects are, many economists now argue that redistributive effects are a relevant policy consideration.[7] Certainly they should be at least specified as far as possible for the decision maker whether or not they are actually included in the calculation of total costs (or benefits).

Assuming that external costs, redistributive effects, and other economic costs can be identified, there remains the measurement problem. Most governmental activities involve both resources and services that are not priced in the open market. Thus, there is no market mechanism that determines the social value of resources used in government programs. One solution is shadow pricing.[8] In effect, the relevant price for a government service is a private sector near-equivalent. For many investment type projects the imputation is a reasonable one. The cost of government-provided electric power easily can be compared with the cost of privately produced power. In that case the government is charged with the full cost even though it has some advantages over private industry that would make the budget costs or actual outlays somewhat lower.

Where no comparable service exists outside government, however, the problem is more difficult. One approach has been to simulate a competitive market for the public service and then estimate the price that would result. Simulation is not a well developed technique in this area, however, and is therefore of limited practical utility.[9] Still, the public sector has long experience with the cost side of the budget and cost estimations are therefore usually reliable.

Budget Costs

Budget costs involve the actual resources used in carrying out a particular policy. Manpower, materials, facilities, and other such resources usually are easily translated into dollar cost figures. An essential element in making this translation is the presence of reliable historical cost data that provide a reservoir of experience upon which cost estimation of proposed programs or program alternatives can be based.

The basic and also most difficult problem in the use of the budget cost estimates is the choice of cost measures to be used. The measure of cost, regardless of the measure used, is really an index in that no single measure of costs includes all relevant cost information. Two basic cost measures are applicable: First, one could use acquisition costs plus operating costs over the life of the program being analyzed. Acquisition costs include research, development, and investment costs. Operating costs cover the cost of operating the program over the assumed period of time it will be in operation. The actual choice of time will depend upon the substantive area being considered as well as the advancement in technology. There is no reason why traditional five-or ten-year planning periods should be automatically assumed in making operating cost estimates.

The second cost measure is basically the same as the first except that rather than using straight acquisition costs, adjusted acquisition costs are used. By adjusted acquisition costs what is meant is that the residual value of the investment is subtracted from the original acquisition cost. This residual value is determined by the value of the use that can be made of the original investment of resources after the period ends for which effectiveness is being measured. In effect, it is the estimated salvage value of resources not totally consumed during the life span of the program. For high capital investment type programs, this concept is relevant whereas for others it may be ignored. This approach is applicable mainly in those situations in which alternative programs or systems are being compared and the original system investments have different life spans. The problem of investment life span will be applicable, for the most part, to those substantive areas in which there are large capital investments.

There are several basic cost factors that should be considered regardless of which one of these costs measures is used.[10]

1. Inheritance—There are times when it is possible to borrow or use part or all of a present ongoing system in carrying out one or more of the alternatives being considered. The value of such preexisting facilities or resources is not normally considered a budget cost. It should be noted that there are still opportunity costs associated with "inherited" resources since use for one program precludes the same use for a different program. If it can be argued, however, that an inherited resource will not be "used up" or reduced in value, then it legitimately may be ignored as either a budget or economic cost. A previously developed technology such as a

computer software package need not be continuously counted a cost every time it is utilized on a new program.

2. Research and Development—The term research and development is used to include basic research, applied research, and development that have been defined respectively as follows: *Basic research* is aimed at developing a fuller knowledge and understanding of the subject under study; *applied research* is directed toward the practical application of new knowledge and usually has specific commercial or public objectives with respect to its output or process. While this is true of applied research, there is also a hope of gaining new scientific knowledge in a systematic manner to the production of useful materials, system, or systems.

Estimating R and D costs poses serious problems since one is never certain in advance how difficult the R and D objective may be. There are some models in use which specify functional relationships among the various aspects of research and development as well as investment and operating costs. They break down the R and D process into several phases, and once the first phase is completed, it is possible to predict the costs of remaining phases. These cost estimation models have been shown to be highly reliable for some types of R and D, but are beyond the scope of this chapter.[11] Regardless of the model that is used for cost estimating there are two statements that can be made regarding research and development costs: The greater the desired advance in the state of the art of the technology, the greater the uncertainty of achieving it, and thus the lower the level of confidence in the research and development cost estimate.

3. Inputs—In costing out inputs one moves into the traditional cost-accounting approach based on the concept of market values. Included in these inputs are those factors representing labor, materials, and entrepreneurship. Besides these costs, the pro rata share of administration and distribution costs must also be considered. Costs may be considered both in terms of time and output. It is therefore possible to talk about total cost, and marginal cost as well as short-run and long-run costs. In the short run some costs are variable and some costs will be fixed; in the long run by definition all costs are variable.

The idea of marginal cost becomes important in trying to determine optimal size of any one alternative or combination of alternatives. Optimal return occurs at the point where marginal cost equals marginal return or where the marginal net return is zero. In dealing with a mixture of alternatives, optimal results occur when all alternatives yield the same marginal return per unit of cost. Therefore, marginal cost and marginal return data are extremely important in any cost analysis.

Another consideration in looking at costs as a function of output is the period involved. If there are fixed costs involved, cost estimates will be made for the short-run period. In dealing with the theory of the firm, short run occurs in the situation where the plant is already a reality and the goal is to run that plant in an optimal manner. There are many instances in government where the decision maker is faced with an analogous situation. In these cases some of the factors he has to deal with are fixed and his problem is to operate at a level of optimal effectiveness given these fixed factors. In the long-run situation no factors are fixed and the analyst can vary all factors to achieve optimal effectiveness. The analyst must be aware of the effect of long-run and short-run effects on his analysis and should make them explicit.

4. Geographic Location—Location will have an effect on the costs of most factors used in any given program. There is a difference in cost among North and South, East, and West, as well as between urban and rural areas. In some cases labor is more costly in one area while capital material will be less costly. Furthermore, there may be a difference in costs between two large urban areas within one state. If the analysis is being done at the federal level, more than just the geographical area of the United States must be considered for some programs. Tables of geographic differences in construction costs have been prepared for these situations.[12]

Results Measurement

As already distinguished at the outset, results are stated in terms of dollars in cost-benefit analysis and nonmonetary measures of effect in cost-effectiveness analysis. Just as there are problems in the measurement of economic and budget costs, similar problems plague the measurement of results. There are externalities on the benefit or results side just as on the cost side. While there is a tendency to think of externalities as costs imposed on parties not directly concerned with a particular program, some parties are indirectly benefited as a result of public expenditures. While there might be a tendency to favor public spending by failing to consider negative or cost externalities, failure to take into account benefits for third parties underestimates the value of public investments.

Assuming that benefits are susceptible to pricing in dollar terms, no special measurement problems arise since the concept of a dollar, or monetary value in general, is well understood. Capital investment programs are often well conceptualized in terms of monetary return. The discussion of shadow pricing in the cost section above is, of course, equally relevant to estimating the monetary value of benefits. Many benefits of public sector programs, however, are susceptible to measurement only in nonmonetary terms.

Where the results are not to be assessed strictly in dollar terms, the measurement problem may be less severe in the sense that one does not have to place a monetary value on the results once measured. Any good measure of effectiveness must be (1) explicitly related to the specified program objectives, and (2) measurable in the sense of replicable. In the measurement of public sector results, many times a trade-off must be made in achieving these two objectives. Especially in the human services areas, the most relevant measures are the most difficult to measure and vice versa. Since in cost-effectiveness analysis the analyst is faced with a situation in which output is not measured in dollar terms, program objectives are often stated in somewhat ambiguous political or normative judgments. For the analyst, the problem is one of first converting these normative judgments into appropriate measures of effectiveness before the assessment of what alternative program outputs are needed to accomplish the desired goals can begin.

For example, in the mental and physical health area the government goal could be stated as follows:

To provide an environment in which hazards to physical and mental health are minimized; to provide means for the prevention of physical and mental disabilities; and to support a system of health care which will assure the availability of health services to those in need of them.

These goals must be converted into specific sets of objectives, such objectives being stated in terms of effects either on individuals and/or environment. These stated effects or impacts are the variables for which effectiveness measures must be developed. In terms of the decision maker it is these impact variables that are of importance and not the output measures that are so commonly reported. For the analyst it is the causal relationship between outputs and impacts that is important because effectiveness is measured at the program impact level while costs are determined at the program output level. Without this impact information it is impossible to make an informed meaningful resource allocation decision.

The problem then in developing adequate measures of effectiveness is to determine those conditons of human behavior or the environment that will indicate to the observer the state of the mental and physical health system. Traditional measures that have been used are such things as morbidity and mortality rates. For the analyst the first question must be relevance of the measure and not availability of data. The second problem for the analyst is determining which output or groups of outputs will bring about the desired changes in the conditions of human behavior and/or the environment that have been determined as measuring the state of the mental and physical health system.

The primary problem for the analyst in developing effectiveness measures, however, is that one is often forced to rely upon data collected by someone else for purposes other than the analysis at hand. Frequently, due to time or cost or both constraints, the analyst is not in a position to develop his own operational effectiveness measures of program objectives. The usual recourse then is to utilize data series regularly collected by other parties. This is characteristic of analyses of economic behavior, but it is equally common to use vital health statistics, crime statistics, basic social, housing, and other census data. Problems in the use of such so-called social indicators cannot be detailed here,[13] but several cautions are included in following paragraphs.

It should be obvious that in using data collected by someone other than the analyst, one suffers from the same lack of reliability in the original measurement process. Federal statistical series may ordinarily be relied upon in that sense, but many nonfederal statistical series related especially to metropolitan areas may be deficient. The only defense the analyst has, however, is to be aware of the problem and to try to determine from the original source what, if any, steps were taken to assess the reliability of the series in the first place.

The question of validity becomes a double problem in using data collected by someone else. One may question whether the data really represents the underlying concepts as intended by the original source as well as question whether the data represents the present

analyst's underlying concepts. Albert Biderman has dealt exten-
sively with the first problem utilizing the FBI's Index of Crimes as
the basic example.[14] He points out that thefts of just over $50 are
given equal weight with kidnapping, murder, and other serious
crimes in computing the overall index. One might obviously question, then, whether an increase in the crime rate as measured by the
index is measuring an increase in crime or merely the effects of
inflation in increasing the value of former petty thefts (below $50) to
over $50. The point is that the measure may not be valid even for its
originally intended purpose. Unless the analyst can disaggregate and
reconstruct the original series to suit his own needs, he may be
caught in this double bind of being unsure of the data's original
validity and of the validity of its use for his purposes. Again, the only
real defense is knowledge of the original purposes for the data
collection and of the procedures used in constructing any aggregate
indices.

Another problem in using data collected by someone else for
other purposes relates to the question of levels of aggregation. Data
may already be aggregated to a level of abstraction inappropriate for
the level of behavior the analyst wishes to understand. The classic
problem is data aggregated by geographic place such as most census
data. The analyst who wishes to explain the behavior of individual
human beings is in a different position if the primary data he has is
already aggregated into larger units such as census tracts, wards,
precincts, cities, or other groupings. The analyst can often only be
conscious of the problem and refrain from inferring the behavior of
individuals from data aggregated at a higher level of abstraction.

In spite of the cautionary tone of these paragraphs, however, it
should be understood that they are intended by the authors not to
dissuade the public official or the academician from undertaking
analysis when conditions are less than ideal, but only to make clear
some of the more obvious sources of error. In many cases the
analyst can develop his own effectiveness measures which may be
used independently of other previously collected data or in a complementary fashion to cross-validate his findings.

Application of the Discount Rate

The discussion in this section is limited to the special problem of the
discount rate. It is separated into a special section both because it is

a controversial question and because the material presented is of a more complex nature than that in preceeding sections.

The characteristic of most public sector investments is that they incur costs and benefits over a period longer than one year, and the pattern of costs and benefits often differ. For most investment type projects, including many investments in so-called human capital such as health and education, the heaviest concentration of cost comes early in the life span of the project, tapering off in later periods. Benefits are normally negligible in the early period, rising rapidly to some peak, then leveling off through the remaining life of the project.

The problem, thus, is that society pays early and reaps the benefits late. Since the question for analysis is whether to undertake a project at all or which of several projects is preferred, it is apparent that generally speaking, benefits are preferred earlier and costs later. Given this preference by most human beings, the longer one waits for benefits, the less value they have for him. To take this preference into account in comparing alternative projects, some means must be devised of reducing benefits by an increasing amount the further they occur in the future.

This device for taking into account time preferences is known as the discount rate. If the benefits of a project, appropriately discounted to reflect the fact that gratification is being postponed, exceed the costs (economic costs), then the program is economically worthwhile. In comparison with other programs or other alternatives, the amount by which benefits exceed costs is the more important factor. A ratio of costs to benefits would be misleading in the sense that differences in the magnitude of different alternatives would be obscured. For example, a program costing $1,000,000 with benefits valued at $1,500,000 would have the same benefit/cost ratio, 1.5, as one costing $10,000,000 with benefits valued at $15,000,000. Unless the $10,000,000 figure exceeds a budget constraint, the latter program is clearly preferable since it yields $5,000,000 in benefits compared with only $500,000 for the former.

The choice of a discount rate to determine these current values, however, presents something of a problem. Too low a rate artificially overstates the value of the public investment whereas too high a rate unfairly reduces the estimated value of the public investment project. In the private sector, the current market rate of interest is a ready guide to investment decisions. An investment project to be economically worthwhile to a firm must yield a rate of return higher than the current interest rate, otherwise the cost of capital exceeds the expected return on that capital invested.

Several alternatives have been suggested as an appropriate discount rate for public expenditure decisions. One that has been used for waterway transportation projects is based on the ". . . average rate of interest payable by the Treasury on interest bearing marketable securities with an original maturity of 15 years or more."[15] This would be the rate reflecting the cost of government borrowing and, in effect, should reflect the opportunity costs of otherwise utilizing the funds. The principal weakness of any government borrowing rate, however, is that both revenue from borrowing and revenue from tax sources are mixed together, and it is not really clear that particular programs are financed from particular revenue sources. An exception is a particular municipal capital investment to be financed by issuance of bonds. To be economically worthwhile, the value of the social returns from that investment should obviously exceed the costs of the project; in that case, the borrowing rate would serve as a reasonable discount rate.

A further problem with using the government borrowing rate as the discount rate is that this rate does not include any element of risk. In the private sector, interest rates reflect in part the possibility of default. They must be sufficiently high to cover the percentage of loans that are not completely repaid. In the public sector there is obviously no concern for default at the federal level and very little real concern that states or municipalities will fail. However, risk in the public sector might be conceptualized in terms of a probability that the benefits of a program will actually be less than what was estimated or expected. Taking this risk, however low or high the probability might be, into account, the discount rate would be in excess of the government borrowing rate. A rate that includes an element of risk is, of course, the average private sector rate; this too has been suggested as suitable for public expenditure decisions. The basic problem with this rate, however, is that it includes risk elements (risk of default, for example) not relevant to public expenditures.

The theoretical argument for setting the discount rate is based on the previously discussed notion of opportunity costs. A public investment is economically efficient only if it does not displace more worthwhile investments, in terms of economic return, in the private sector. The appropriate discount rate is, therefore, the rate of return on private sector investments.[16] William J. Baumol illustrates the application of the opportunity cost criterion succinctly:

If the resources in question produce a rate of return in the private sector which society evaluates at r percent, then the resources should be transferred to the public project if that project yields a return greater than r percent. They should be left in private hands if their potential earnings in the proposed government investment is less than r percent. The logic of this criterion is self-evident. It states no more than the minimal dictate of efficiency: Never take resources out of a use where they bring in (say) 9 percent in order to utilize them in a manner which yields only 6 percent.[17]

The immediate problem with attempting to use the private sector market rate is that there are numerous private sector rates. Furthermore, the opportunity cost of capital differs depending on whether the source of the capital is the consumer or the corporate component of the economy. Several factors, including differentials in risk taxation, account for these differences.

The use of a private market rate, however accurately determined, is questioned on grounds other than the measurement problem. In general, consumers tend to prefer immediate rather than long-term satisfaction that would tend to disfavor public investments. Likewise, corporate decisions involve greater elements of risks, plus they are more restricted to the necessity for returning a profit; thus, both the consumer and corporate components of the private sector would tend to produce a high discount rate. This high discount rate would work to the advantage of public sector investments, which might be desirable for social reasons. Social security, for example, is perhaps an instance where the social returns are of more importance than the economic returns.

The discount rate problem is not hopeless. A concern for setting a rate that does not overvalue public investments is important. Studies have shown that varying the rate between 4 and 8 percent does not really make any difference in the evaluation of a project.[18] Given that the analysts role is one of supplying information to decision makers rather than making the decisions according to one particular criterion such as economic efficiency, it would seem appropriate that three alternative discount rates be used—one high, one medium, and one low. In this situation, the analyst is making clear the effects of varying assumptions about the present value of future benefits and costs without arbitrarily assigning a single discount rate that yields a seemingly inescapable conclusion to adopt or not adopt a particular project.

Although the discount rate problem is normally limited to cost-benefit analysis, the conceptual problem is equally relevant to cost-effectiveness analysis. Even though results may be measured in nonmonetary terms, the farther into the future they occur, the less value they presently have. In some sense, the time pattern of costs and results, whether measured as dollars or other results, should be taken into account. In a cost-effectiveness analysis, this might take the form of simply displaying the level of expected results (and costs) over time. Costs and results might have to be displayed on separate graphs since the unit of measurement for the vertical axis would naturally differ, but some form of display should be undertaken. Then alternative projects might at least be compared visually. If the results of several alternatives are measured in the same unit (lives saved or accidents averted, for example), and they occur in different patterns over time for each of the alternatives, it would then be possible to determine the most valuable projects taking into account both absolute magnitude of results and time.

Conclusions

In the preceding sections much of the focus was on rather complex problems in identifying and measuring relevant costs and benefits. Lest the analyst, whether academic or practitioner, be misled into thinking that only analysis that solves all of these problems is useful analysis, this section argues that economic analysis ranges from the simple to the complex. Depending on the susceptibility of the programs or program alternatives to quantitative measurement, the skills of the analyst, and the amount of resources available for impact analysis, economic analysis may be highly quantitative or it may be heavily qualitative and descriptive. The key feature of economic analysis, whether it be of the cost-benefit or the cost-effectiveness variety, is that it focuses decision making on questions of the relationship between costs and results. Any analysis that examines program alternatives as a range of choices that imply other opportunities foregone is rightfully considered economic analysis. In that sense, economic analysis is always a comparative analysis.

While theoretical economists may be more concerned with establishing criteria for determining the proper allocation of resources between the private and public sectors, program analysts are normally more concerned with choices solely within the public sector. The alternatives normally subjected to economic analysis are all within the public sector. Even restricted to the public sector, however, the economic analysis of alternatives focuses on important questions of efficiency and equity. At the state government level, alternative programs may involve the difference between providing certain services at the state level or requiring municipal governments to provide those services. The most important question in that analysis may be on the cost side, specifically on how the costs are distributed among the people of the state. Most state governments have broader based tax sources than do local governments. The distribution of costs of the two alternatives, given different tax bases, would place the economic burden differently on segments of the population. On the results side, variations in the abilities of different municipal governments to provide the particular service may mean an uneven distribution of benefits among the total state population even if costs are spread equitably by financing the service at the state level.

Primary candidates for increased use of analysis in general and economic analysis in particular are the thousands of local governments. Even with limited resources, analysis can contribute to improving the quality of local government decision making even if only by making explicit comparisons of existing programs with alternatives foregone. The biggest step in conducting systematic analysis at the local government level may be the reorganization of existing data collection. Local governments already systematically collect large amounts of data relevant to the conduct of particular services. This data, however, relates almost exclusively to workload type statistics. In a study of solid waste collection conducted by The Urban Institute, the common measures of operation were observed:

1. Tons or cubic yards of waste collected
2. Frequency of service
3. Number of special-request collections
4. Tons collected per man-hour
5. Miles of streets cleaned
6. Collections per crew[19]

While each of these measures may be important for operational purposes, none of them contributes data directly to questions of effectiveness or results.

In their recommendations, The Urban Institute staff team suggested two general objectives that they found to be implicit in most waste collection programs:

1. Promoting the health, safety, and aesthetics of the community by providing an environment free from the hazards and unpleasantness of uncollected solid wastes
2. Reducing the amount of inconvenience and danger to residents and businesses in handling and disposing of their own wastes[20]

Table 13-2 below lists the eight measures of effectiveness that the study recommended be adopted as indications of program success in accomplishing the more general objectives. Of the eight, only the last, Index of Citizen Dissatisfaction, requires extensive data collection beyond institutional records that already are kept by some jurisdictions or could easily be maintained. Some of the barriers to utilizing existing data sources are only the fact that relevant departments are not always notified—for example, of citizen complaints about noise or damage reports.

Costs for existing programs in solid waste collection would, of course, already be maintained. Should measurement of some or all of the indicators of program impact in Table 13-2 show the need for improvement of basic services, economic analysis would serve to focus attention on comparative costs and results of alternative changes in the existing program. Although a cost analysis of changes in a solid waste collection program might show such changes to be feasible, focusing attention on economic costs raises the question of whether changes in the solid waste program, however, beneficial, are more worthwhile than alternative uses for the funds that would have to be foregone. Thus, economic analysis not only focuses attention on the relationship between costs and results, but it does so in a wider comparative framework.

In summary, problems of economic analysis are not insurmountable. The complexities of analysis should be understood primarily in order to introduce a note of caution into naive analyses purporting to give the decision maker the one, unique, and correct answer.

Table 13-2
Basic Measures of Solid Waste Collection Effectiveness

Health and Safety Measures
1. Rate of observed health hazards and injuries to waste collectors
2. Rate of observed fire hazards and the number of fires involving uncollected wastes

Aesthetics Measures
3. Rate of observed unsightly appearances
4. Rate of offensive odors
5. Number of objectionable noise incidents

Citizen Inconvenience and Property Loss Measures
6. Index of inconvenience
7. Index of damages occurring during collection

General Public Satisfaction Measures
8. Index of citizen dissatisfaction

Source: "Measuring the Effectiveness of Local Government Services: Solid Waste Collection," Louis H. Blair, Harry P. Hatry, Pasqual A. Don Vito (Washington, D.C.: The Urban Institute, October 1970), p. 9.

Notes

1. Gene H. Fisher, "The Role of Cost-Utility Analysis in Program Budgeting," in *Planning Programming Budgeting: A Systems Approach to Management* (Chicago: Markham, 1968), pp. 181-98.

2. Charles L. Schultz, "Why Benefit-Cost Analysis?" in *Program Budgeting and Benefit-Cost Analysis* (Pacific Palisades, California: Goodyear Publishing Co., 1969), pp. 2-3.

3. Karl Seiler, *Introduction to Systems Cost-Effectiveness* (New York: John Wiley & Sons, 1969), p. 1.

4. William A. Niskanen, "Measures of Effectiveness," in *Cost-Effectiveness Analysis: New Approaches in Decision-Making* (New York: Praeger Publishers, 1968), p. 18.

5. Kenneth E. Boulding, *Economic Analysis: Micro Economics* (New York: Harper & Row Publishers, 1966), p. 303.

6. A.R. Prest and R. Turvey, "Cost-Benefit Analysis: A Survey," *The Economic Journal* 75 (1965), pp. 683-735.

7. Burton A. Weisbrod, "Income Redistribution Effects and

Benefit-Cost Analysis," in *Problems in Public Expenditure Analysis* (Washington: Brookings Institution, 1968), pp. 177-208.

8. Julius Margolis, "Shadow Prices for Incorrect or Nonexistent Market Values," in Subcommittee on Economy in Government, *The Analysis and Evaluation of Public Expenditures* (Washington: Brookings Institution, 1969), pp. 533-46. Roland N. McKean, "The Use of Shadow Prices," in *Problems in Public Expenditure Analysis* (Washington: Brookings Institution, 1968), pp. 33-65.

9. McKean, "The Use of Shadow Prices."

10. Seiler, *Introduction to Systems Cost-Effectiveness.*

11. Ibid.

12. Ibid.

13. Raymond A. Bauer, *Social Indicators* (Cambridge: MIT Press, 1966).

14. Albert D. Biderman, "Social Indicators and Goals," in Bauer, *Social Indicators.*

15. Robert L. Banks and Arnold Kotz, "The Program Budget and The Interest Rate for Public Investment," *Public Administration Review* 26 (1966).

16. William J. Baumol, "On the Discount Rate for Public Projects," in *Public Expenditures and Public Analysis* (Chicago: Markham, 1970), pp. 273-90.

17. Ibid., p. 274.

18. C.D. Foster and M.E. Beesley, cited in Prest and Turvey, "Cost-Benefit Analysis."

19. Louis H. Blair, Harry P. Hatry, and Pasqual A. Don Vito, *Measuring the Effectiveness of Local Government Services: Solid Waste Collection* (Washington: The Urban Institute, 1970).

20. Ibid.

Indexes

Index of Authors

Index of Subjects

About the Contributors

Herbert B. Asher is associate professor of political science at Ohio State University. He received the Ph.D. from the University of Michigan in 1970. He is the author of a number of articles on the socialization of freshmen congressmen, legislative politics, policy analysis, and political methodology that have appeared in such journals as the *American Political Science Review*, *American Journal of Political Science*, *Annals*, *Political Methodology*, and *Sage Professional Papers in American Politics*.

David A. Caputo is associate professor of political science at Purdue University. He is the author of *American Politics and Public Policy: An Introduction* and "Organized Crime in America," and a coauthor, with Richard L. Cole, of *Urban Politics and Decentralization: The Case of General Revenue Sharing*. He has published in the *Midwest Journal of Politics*, *Public Administration Review*, *Urban Affairs Quarterly*, *Publius*, the *1974 Municipal Yearbook*, and the *Policy Studies Journal*. Dr. Caputo received the Ph.D. from Yale University in 1970.

Thomas R. Dye is professor of government at Florida State University. He obtained the Ph.D. from the University of Pennsylvania. He is past secretary of the American Political Science Association and president-elect of the Southern Political Science Association. Dr. Dye's most recent text is *Understanding Public Policy* (1972).

James W. Dyson is associate professor of government at Florida State University. He received the Ph.D. from Indiana University. His main research interests are in the application of experimental design to the study of political phenomena. Dr. Dyson is cofounder and coeditor of the journal *Experimental Study of Politics*.

Virginia Gray is assistant professor of political science at the University of Minnesota; she taught previously at the University of Kentucky. She has published in the *American Political Science Review*, the *American Journal of Political Science*, *Journal of American History*, *Polity*, and she has edited (with Elihu Bergman) the book *Political Issues in U.S. Population Policy*.

Ronald W. Johnson is assistant professor of political science at the Pennsylvania State University. He received the Ph.D. from the State University of New York at Buffalo. He is a coauthor, with Robert D. Lee, Jr., of *Public Budgeting Systems*, and he has contributed to scholarly journals specializing in public policy issues and analysis. Dr. Johnson is an organizational development consultant to the New York Metropolitan Area YMCAs and the National Board of the YWCA.

E. Terrence Jones is an associate professor of political science at the University of Missouri-St. Louis. He is the author of *Conducting Political Research* (1971), and his articles on policy evaluation, urban politics, and electoral behavior have appeared in such journals as *American Politics Quarterly*, *Criminology*, *Experimental Study of Politics*, *Social Indicators Research*, *Urban Affairs Quarterly*, and *Western Political Quarterly*.

Eugene J. Meehan is professor of political science at the University of Missouri-St. Louis. He obtained the Ph.D. from the London School of Economics. His books include *Explanation and Social Science* (1968), *Value Judgment and Social Science* (1969), and *Foundations of Political Analysis* (1971). Dr. Meehan previously taught at the University of Illinois, Brandeis University, and Rutgers University.

Stuart S. Nagel is professor of political science at the University of Illinois and a member of the Illinois bar. He is the author of *Improving the Legal Process: Effects of Alternatives* (1975), *Environmental Politics* (1974), *The Rights of the Accused: In Law and Action* (1972), and *The Legal Process from a Behavioral Perspective* (1969). Dr. Nagel has been a visiting fellow at the LEAA National Institute, Yale Law and Social Science Program, the East-West Center, and the Center for Advanced Study in the Behavioral Sciences.

Elinor Ostrom is professor of political science and codirector of the Workshop in Political Theory and Policy Analysis at Indiana University. She received the Ph.D. from the University of California at Los Angeles. She is involved in a National Science Foundation

(RANN Division) grant investigation 200 metropolitan areas, entitled "Evaluating the Organization of Service Delivery: Police."

John M. Pierce is an assistant professor in the Department of Humanities, Department of Behavioral Science in the College of Medicine, the Pennsylvania State University. He received the Ph.D. from the Pennsylvania State University and the J.D. from the University of Denver. He previously taught at Michigan State University and the University of Wyoming College of Law. Dr. Pierce is the author of articles relating public policy to medicine and of *Resources Handbook: Planning, Zoning and Related Laws*. He is also a consultant in the field of health policy.

Neumann Pollock is assistant professor of political science at Oakland University. He received the Ph.D. from Florida State University, where his dissertation concerned public policy.

Douglas St. Angelo is associate professor of government at Florida State University. He received the Ph.D. from the University of Chicago. He is the author of *Cooperation and Conflict: Dynamics of American Federalism* (1969) and has published articles in major research journals.

Donald S. Van Meter is assistant professor of political science at Ohio State University. He received the Ph.D. from the University of Wisconsin in 1972. He is the author of a number of articles on policy analysis and political methodology that have appeared in such journals as *Administration and Society*, *Policy Studies Journal*, *Political Methodology*, and *Sage Professional Papers in American Politics*. Dr. Van Meter is also the coauthor, with Ira Sharkansky, of *Policy and Politics in American Governments*.

L.A. Wilson II is a candidate for the Ph.D. in political science at the University of Oregon. He is a research felollow at the Oregon Research Institute in Eugene, Oregon, and at the Center for Educational Policy and Management at the University of Oregon. He is the coauthor of several articles that have appeared in *Urban Affairs Quarterly* and *Comparative Political Studies*. Mr. Wilson's major interests are in the areas of public policy analysis, urban politics, and methodology.

About the Editors

Frank P. Scioli, Jr., is associate professor of Political Science at the University of Illinois at Chicago Circle and Director of the Ph.D. program in public policy analysis. He received the Ph.D. from Florida State University in 1970 and formerly taught at Drew University. A consultant to federal, state, and local agencies, he was coprincipal investigator of a National Science Foundation (RANN Division) grant, which produced the monograph *The Effectiveness of Volunteer Programs in Courts and Corrections: An Evaluation of Policy Related Research* (1975). Dr. Scioli has published in numerous social science journals. He is coeditor and cofounder of the *Experimental Study of Politics* and of the *Policy Studies Journal.*

Thomas J. Cook is associate professor of political science at the University of Illinois at Chicago Circle. He received the Ph.D. from Florida State University in 1969, and taught at Pennsylvania State University before joining the faculty at Chicago Circle. He was coprincipal investigator, with Dr. Scioli, of the monograph listed above and has served as a consultant on program evaluation to federal, state, and local governments. Dr. Cook serves on the editorial boards of the *Experimental Study of Politics* and the *Policy Studies Journal*, and he has published in numerous social science journals.